শ্রীমন্নামামৃতসিন্ধুবন্দু

The Nectar of the Holy Name

Manindranath Guha

Introduced, translated, and annotated
by
Neal Delmonico

Blazing Sapphire Press
715 E. McPherson Street
Kirksville, MO 63501 (USA)

ISBN 978-0-9747968-1-9 (Soft-cover)
ISBN 978-0-9747968-2-6 (Hardcover)

Published by:
Blazing Sapphire Press
715 E. McPherson Street
Kirksville, Missouri 63501
(USA)

Distributed by:
Nitai's Bookstore
715 E. McPherson Street
Kirksville, Missouri 63501
Phone: (660) 665-0273
Email: ndelmonico@sbcglobal.net
http://www.blazingsapphirepress.com
http://www.nitaisbookstore.com

Contents

Acknowledgments

It is with great pleasure that I recognize all of those friends without whose help this book would not have been completed. My thanks go to Joseph Knapp for his support and encouragement during the final stages of this project. Without that little added push, this translation might never have been completed and without his financial support for the project the translation, though finished, might never have seen the light of day. Joseph also contributed the Preface, helped proofread the final proofs and read through an earlier draft of the translation, giving many useful suggestions on how to improve it. I would also like to thank Lynn Shook who took valuable time out of her busy schedule to read parts of the draft and point out numerous ways in which it might be improved. My heart-felt thanks go to her. Mark Tinghino also deserves credit for his contribution to the work by giving it a careful read and final fine-tuning of the language and grammar of the translation. Last but not least my deep appreciation goes to my wife Betsy who not only encouraged me to continue when my enthusiasm for the work was flagging, but who also read through the manuscript not once but numerous times and made countless corrections and suggestions for text's improvement. Without her help and support, this translation would certainly never have gotten off the ground.

Acknowledgments

[illegible]

Preface

I first met Manindranath Guha in 1979 at a celebration at the temple of my *gurudeva*, Śrī Śrī 108 Tin Kuḍi Goswami. I could not help but notice him — he stood out by his bright countenance. We talked and soon became friends. I fondly remember all the times he gave *pāṭha* (reading or recital of one of the sacred texts) during the holy month of Kartika (October-November) at Bābā's place in Radhakunda. Although I could only understand twenty-five percent of what he said — he impressed me with the intensity and concentrated focus he brought to the performance of the customary *pūjā* and *mantra* recitations before the beginning of the reading and equally while reciting the text and giving explanations, his elucidations of the text.

He became like an older brother to me and the brotherly affection he showed me went a long way towards making me feel more comfortable and at home living in Vraja with Bābā. Life with Bābā and the other *bābājīs* as we moved from holy place to holy place in Vraja was rather hard, but at the same time blissful.

At times I would spend several days at Manibabu's house on my occasional trips to Vrindaban. It was wonderful to hear him each morning recite his 100,000 (one *lakh* or *lakṣa*) Holy Names, all in one sitting. He did this each and every morning out loud without fail and then he would continue with the other spiritual practices as they are performed in our tradition. When one lives in the company of the *bābājis* one tends to recite the Holy Name (Mantra Meditation) either quietly to ourselves (*upāṃśu*) or silently in the mind (*mānasika*) — can you imagine five or ten *bābājis* doing their mantra recitations out loud — not the best circumstance for concentration.[1]

[1] To accomplish the repetition of a hundred thousand Holy Names we use a *mālā* (string

Whether we are renunciants, students, married or retired, of Eastern birth or Western birth, those of us who are in this tradition of *mantra* recitation are guided by the great Luminary of India Śrī Caitanya Mahāprabhu to recite 100,000 Holy Names each and every day. By doing so ALL will be attained, ALL will be accomplished, ALL will be loved, appreciated, and glorified. We try to do this when sitting down in a meditation posture in one or two sittings within a twenty-four hour time period. We do this with the utmost love, concentrated focus, and with respect and humility. Done in this way, our lives become blessed in ways most people cannot comprehend. We experience the thrill of drinking the elixir of concentrated being, consciousness, and bliss (*sat-cid-ananda*). *Kṛṣṇa-prema-bhakti* is an experience of such closeness to God — to Śrī Kṛṣṇa — and its bestowal is a direct, compassionate response from Nāma Prabhu (the Holy Name).

It is a matter of great pleasure and satisfaction for me to see that this English translation of Mr. Guha's work will now be available to the English-speaking public. For the first time the western world will be exposed to this important text on one of the great Vaiṣṇava practices, a practice that has been glorified and performed by millions of people in India and other parts of the world for the last 600 (and more) years. Due to the importance of this book's subject matter and for a deeper understanding of it, I suggest this book be read through several times.

We hope that this book will serve as a brief introduction to the much larger books on this important subject that were written by Mr. Guha's

---

of beads usually made from the *tulasī*, sacred basil plant) containing one hundred and eight beads (plus a head bead that is not used in the count, but rather lets us know when we reach it that we have completed a "round" of one hundred and eight repetitions). We repeat a very special mantra (a verbal formula consisting of sacred syllables) called the Great Mantra (Mahāmantra). It is called "great" because anyone can use it and by repeating it can gain great happiness in closeness to God Kṛṣṇa. This Mahāmantra you may have heard before from many different sources. It consists of sixteen names:

Hare Kṛṣṇa Hare Kṛṣṇa Kṛṣṇa Kṛṣṇa Hare Hare
Hare Rāma Hare Rāma Rāma Rāma Hare Hare

This Holy Mahāmantra comes from *Kali-santaraṇa Upaniṣad* where it appears in the reversed order beginning with *Hare Rāma* instead of *Hare Kṛṣṇa*. The Mahāmantra also appears in the *Brahmāṇḍa Purāṇa*, Uttarakhaṇḍa, 6.55, where the order is as it is given here. Śrī Caitanya accepted the form beginning with *Hare Kṛṣṇa* as authentic.

One arrives at one hundred thousand repetitions in the following way: one hundred and eight beads by sixteen names equals 1,728 names. Those multiplied by sixty-four "rounds" equals 110,592 repetitions of the Holy Name (Nāma Prabhu, Master Name). Thus we have one hundred thousand repetitions or recitations and a few extras to make up for loss of concentration, and so forth.

own blessed *dīkṣā-guru*, Śrīman Kanupriya Goswami. These will be translated and published in the (hopefully) near future! Kindly bless the lowly slaves behind these projects. Let us pray for the long life and health of the principal translator Śrī Nitai Dasji, whose scholarly acumen is well known. If anyone should pray for me — let it be that I may somehow get a chance to serve Hari, *guru*, the Vaiṣṇavas and do that in true humility. May I be stripped of everything that comes in the way of that.

With humble sincerity,

Jagadish Das 1-19-2006
Kirksville, MO

Translator's Introduction

I am pleased to be able to present in English Manindranath Guha's classic Bengali work on the theology of the holy name, entitled *Śrīman Nāmāmṛtra-sindhu-bindu* ("A Drop of the Ocean of Nectar of the Holy Name," shortened in this translation to simply *Nectar of the Holy Name*). I began this translation way back in 1977, when I was a student at the University of Colorado, Boulder. I had just returned to the United States from India and gone back to college to complete my undergraduate degree. I had dropped out of the university some seven years earlier to explore a form of cultural and religious alterity, immersing myself in Caitanya Vaiṣṇavism as a member of the Hare Krishna Movement. After more than six good years in the International Society for Krishna Consciousness (ISKCON), I left it in search of a less westernized form of Caitanya Vaiṣṇavism. What I found among the renunciant *babas* (hermits) of Vraja is the Vaiṣṇava world that is reflected in Manindranath Babu's little book. His work was one of the many Bengali and Sanskrit jewels I discovered around the time of my departure from ISKCON and it exerted a powerful influence on me at that transformative time of my life.

My translation of Manindranath's book began as part of a research project for a course of independent study I took on Hinduism at the University of Colorado, a course in which I was guided by Dr. Robert Lester. I believe I only translated the first ten or fifteen pages for that project and after the course was complete I put it aside for a several years, hardly even thinking of it again. My interest in the text was re-ignited, however, when I met Manindranath Babu again, probably in 1985 when I was in India, this time for my doctoral research as a graduate student of the University of Chicago. At that time he gave me (or I purchased from him) a copy of the much enlarged second edition of this book. This larger edition became the basis of the translation presented here.

The Author and His Other Works

I had the good fortune of meeting Manindranath Guha several times in and around Vrindaban during the years that I lived or visited there. I don't remember when we first met, but I do recall that on several occasions he graciously invited me to his house for chats and to participate in *kīrtana*, the singing of Kṛṣṇa's names. I was never able to take him up on the offer and I profoundly regret that today. It would have given me much more insight into him, his book, and the religious practices and studies out of which this book grew. As it is, what I am about to present of his life and practice I have learned from others who knew him, from hints in his books, and from my recollection of his own stray comments on those few occasions when we had a chance to talk at more length. I apologize to his family and relatives if I have gotten anything wrong. Unfortunately, he is no longer around for me to apologize to him personally.

Manindranath Guha was a bright, motivated and talented fellow, an engineer by training and profession. On the title pages of his books he refers to himself as a retired, assistant Chief Engineer of the Public Works Department of West Bengal. Thus, he held a rather high and important post in the government of West Bengal, an indication of his ability, drive, and intelligence. His wife's name was Savitri. She had a master's degree in Sanskrit, though I am not sure from which university, and two *tīrthas*, special degrees granted in the traditional Sanskritic education system in India: one in the area of Purāṇic studies and the other in Vaiṣṇava philosophy. I don't know for sure if Manindranath and his wife Savitri had any children, but I believe they did not.

Like so many talented and educated young Bengalis in the first half of the 20th century, he was first drawn to Caitanya Vaiṣṇavism through the proselytizing efforts of the Gauḍīya Math and especially by its charismatic leader Bhaktisiddhanta Sarasvati. When this occurred and for how long, I am not sure. And again like so many of the brightest of those, after the passing of Bhaktisiddhanta he became inspired by exemplary Vaiṣṇavas from the mainstream Vaiṣṇava community, beyond the confines of the Gauḍīya Math organization. Thus, along with great Vaiṣṇava leaders, writers and practitioners like Puridas, Sundarananda Vidyavinoda, Dr. O. B. L. Kapoor, Anantadas Baba (Govindakunda), Kṛṣṇadas Baba (Madrasi), Haripadadasa Baba (Kṛṣṇadas Baba's brother), and many others, Manindranath left the Gauḍīya Math and sought shelter with a teacher (*guru*) from the traditional Vaiṣṇava community. He eventually was accepted as a disciple by Kanupriya Goswami of Nabadwip, who was famed as a great writer and speaker and who was recognized in the Vaiṣṇava community as an exemplary teacher of the "science" of the holy name (*nāma-vijñānācārya*). It was no doubt in large part the influence of Kanupriya Goswami that led Manindranath to write on the theology of the holy name. It is certainly Kanupriya Goswami who he has in mind as the "Goswami" in the dialogue in this book.

After his retirement, Manindranath and his wife eventually settled in Vrindaban, and he began his career as a writer of books on Caitanya Vaiṣṇavism. His first book, the *Śrī Mādhava-mādhurya-mañjuṣā*, "The Treasure Chest of the Sweetness of Mādhava," was published in 1969 by his wife Savitri. Replete with diagrams, charts, lists and of course, numerous quotes from the original Vaiṣṇava scriptures, both in Sanskrit and Bengali, it describes Kṛṣṇa's sport in Vṛndāvana as perhaps only an engineer would dare to, with an eye for detail and schematics. I don't know how good Manindranath's knowledge of Sanskrit was, but although he does not mention it anywhere as far as I know, I am sure his wife, whose knowledge of Sanskrit was apparently quite good, gave him a great deal of assistance with the Sanskrit passages. One of the fine qualities of all of Manindranath's books is the nearly mistake-free citation of long and complicated Sanskrit passages in the footnotes and the high quality of the translations into Bengali of those passages. Manindranath's wife no doubt deserves much of the credit for that.

Encouraged by the success of his first book, Manindranath published his second book in 1971: The *Śrī Gaura-karuṇā-candrikā-kaṇā*, "A Ray of the Moonlight of Gaura's Grace." This book on the life of Śrī Caitanya (Gaura) is even larger than the first book and like the first book is filled with numerous quotations from the old Vaiṣṇava scriptures. It also contains two pictures of Śrī Caitanya drawn by his wife. Manindranath regarded his first two books as the results of his own realizations and insights arising from his study and practice of Caitanya Vaiṣṇavism. He often humbly warned people that this is what they were getting, not a reproduction of a standard work of the Caitanya tradition.

In 1971 Manindranath also published his edition of the *Śrī Caitanya-candrāmṛta*, "Ambrosia of the Moon of Caitanya." by Prabodhānanda Sarasvatī, an early follower of Śrī Caitanya. Included in that edition was the commentary by Ānandi on the text and Manindranath's translation into Bengali of both text and commentary. This was the first of several edition-translations that Manindranath was to publish. Manindranath published yet a third book in that extraordinarily productive year: An edition with a long Bengali commentary of the eight verses of instruction attributed to Śrī Caitanya called the *Śikṣāṣṭaka*, "Eight Instructive Verses." In this book Manindranath presented for the first time the idea, no doubt received from his guru, that the first of those eight verses presents in a nutshell the whole process of the cultivation of *bhakti* as it is envisioned in the Caitanya tradition from the beginning of practice, called *bhajana-kriyā*, to the stage of the "great emotion," *mahābhāva*, said to be the highest stage of the development of divine love, a stage believed to be found only in Śrī Rādhā, Kṛṣṇa's best lover among the cowherd women.

The next book that Manindranath published, in 1975, was an edition of the Sanskrit play by the great Vaiṣṇava poet Kavi Karṇapūra, the *Caitanya-candrodaya*, "The Rise of the Moon of Caitanya," on the life of Śrī Caitanya. This he published with a Sanskrit commentary and his own Bengali translation, again of both text and commentary. After that he published the first edition of the book translated here, the *Śrīman-nāmāmṛta-sindhu-bindu*, "A Drop of the Ocean of Nectar of the Holy Name." It was published in 1976 with the second, longer edition coming out in 1984.

For his next work, Manindranath undertook a huge and difficult task: The editing and translation of Kavi Karṇapūra's masterpiece on Kṛṣṇa's sport in Vṛndāvana, the *Ānanda-vṛndāvana-campū*, "Joyful Vṛndāvana." The first volume came out in 1982 and was eventually followed by the second volume. That work is extremely difficult because of the author's complex and skillful use of puns and double-entendres. It is not uncommon for Karṇapūra to play three levels of meaning, parallel but distinct, off of each other in some places in the poem. A *campū* is a genre of Sanskrit poetic work which mixes passages of prose with verse. One has to admire Manindranath for undertaking not only an edition of the text, but its complete translation into Bengali.

The final work that Manindranath undertook was an edition with commentaries of the Tenth Canto of the *Bhāgavata Purāṇa*. At least three volumes of that work came out before Manindranath passed away. It includes two commentaries, the *Vaiṣṇava-toṣaṇī* of Śrī Jīva and the *Sārārtha-darśinī* of Viśvanātha Cakravartin, again with full translation into Bengali. In this way, Manindranatha and his wife Savitri spent their retirement days living in Vrindaban, and writing, editing, and translating works on Caitanya Vaiṣṇavism.

One of the notable characteristics of Manindranath's books is in the way he includes in all but his first book praises and comments on his various books from many of the great Caitanya Vaiṣṇavas of his day. Those sections of his books, usually found at the back, read almost like a who's who of the great Vaiṣṇava scholars and practitioners of that generation, many of whom have left us no other writings except for the letters they wrote praising Manindranath's books. Great Vaiṣṇavas like Kiśorīkiśorānanda Dāsa Bābā, Nṛsiṃha Vallabha Goswami, Gaurāṅga Dāsa Bābā, Priyācaraṇa Dāsa Bābā, Ananta Das Baba (the current mahanta of Radhakund), to name only a few, have all written glowing reviews of one or another of Manindranath's books. This is a practice that was quite common in Caitanya Vaiṣṇava works written in Bengali earlier in the 20th century. Manindranath's guru, Kanupriya Goswami, for instance, did much the same thing in many of his books, including remarks from the likes of Atulakrishna Goswami, Pranagopal Goswami, Rasikamohan Vidyabhusan, Pramathanath Tarkabhusan, and many others. Several other examples can be cited for this practice.

As far as Manindranath's personal practice of Caitanya Vaiṣṇavism is concerned, I understand that he, without fail, chanted out loud one *lakh* (100,000) of the names of Kṛṣṇa each day in the form of *japa* of the Mahāmantra.[2] In addition to that he sang *kīrtana* for up to two hours a day, just as he recommends in this book. He also remained a householder to the end of his days, never entering the renounced order of life to become what is known in Caitanya Vaiṣṇism as a *bābā* (lit. father). For him the householder life must have seemed perfectly suited for the kind of service he wanted to offer the tradition.

Short Analysis of This Work

Manindranath's book on the holy name is of interest from a number of perspectives. In the first place it is the work of someone I would consider an amateur theologian, as opposed to what might be understood as a professional theologian in the Caitanya Vaiṣṇava tradition. For instance, he was not born into one of the traditional Goswami families for

[2] *Japa* is a type of repetition of the holy names or of a *mantra* that one counts on a rosary or on one's fingers. 100,000 repetitions of Kṛṣṇa's names in the form of the Mahāmantra amounts to 64 rounds on a Vaiṣṇava rosary which contains 108 beads. The Mahāmantra is, of course: *hare kṛṣṇa hare kṛṣṇa kṛṣṇa kṛṣṇa hare hare; hare rāma hare rāma rāma rāma hare hare.*

whom Caitanya Vaiṣṇavism has been a family treasure and tradition for centuries. The word 'Goswami' (Master of Cows) is a title of honor and respect that has become almost a family name for numerous families who trace their ancestry back to the companions and close followers of Śrī Caitanya. While most of those Goswami families have maintained a close connection with the Caitanya tradition and have played important roles in transmitting and preserving the Caitanya tradition down through the centuries, some have not done so and have taken to other religious beliefs or to none at all. Usually, however, someone born into such a family is educated from the ground up in Sanskrit and in the important texts of the tradition. Some among the Goswamis have become well known teachers and writers of the tradition. This is one group that I would consider "professional" theologians.

Nor was Manindranath, as mentioned before, a member of the renunciant community, the "bābājīs." Though the main focus of that community is intense, full-time practice, a few of the members of that community have undertaken careful and detailed studies of various aspects of the Caitanya tradition, acquiring the necessary language skills, in many cases, after becoming members. This group is the other source of "professional" theologians. Manindranath's *Nectar of the Holy Names*, however, is by an enthusiastic follower of the tradition for other enthusiasts or would-be enthusiasts and as such lacks something in systematic and logical organization and presentation. In places it strikes one more as a kind of ejaculation of joyful enthusiasm for the holy name that gets at times a bit preachy and dogmatic and at other times rather repetitive.

The book is written in the form of a dialogue between someone called Laghu (Light-weight) and someone called Goswami. Laghu is no doubt Manindranath himself and Goswami is his guru, Kanupriya Goswami.[3] The dialogue between Laghu and Goswami in this book is probably based on real dialogues between Manindranath and his guru, no doubt expanded, embellished and refined. It is unlikely that Manindranath wrote them down verbatim or that Kanupriya Goswami recited from memory those long passages of commentary from Śrī Sanātana or Śrī Jīva in the course of their discussions together. Kanupriya was indeed a learned man and someone I would consider a professional theologian in the Caitanya tradition. Thus he may have pointed out those passages to Manindranath and left it to him to interpret and apply them properly. Manindranath tells us in his own introduction that his book is the result

---

[3] *Laghu*, light, is the semantic opposite of *guru*, heavy.

of his own reflection (*manana*, thinking over) on what he had heard from his teacher. Some of the passages he uses to support his statements were probably discovered on his own or with the help of his wife. There is a good deal of truth in Manindranath's claim that nothing in his book is his own, that he is merely distributing what is already available in the works of the Gosvāmin of Vṛndāvana. But that is not entirely true. He sometimes adds a little bit here and there of his own interpretation of those works.

The fundamental mission of the book is to encourage a return to what the author views as the basic practices and principles of the Caitanya Vaiṣṇava tradition: the idea that *saṅkīrtana* of the holy names is the only practice one needs in order to cultivate and acquire the highest levels of love for Rādhā and Kṛṣṇa. All other religious practices are secondary to and dependent on the *saṅkīrtana* of the holy names. By *saṅkīrtana*, or complete (*samyak*) recitation (*kīrtana*), Manindranath means, following the opinion of the Gosvāmins, melodically singing the holy names with musical accompaniment. Though this can be done alone, it is best done with others who share one's particular way of relating to Kṛṣṇa. Simple or plain *kīrtana*, on the other hand, is merely loud repetition of Kṛṣṇa's names not necessarily done musically. Manindranath makes the point repeatedly that Śrī Caitanya is the "father of *saṅkīrtana*" and is most pleased when his devotees enthusiastically honor his son.

As mentioned before Manindranath in his book provides support for almost everything he says by citing passages from the works of the Gosvāmins of Vṛndāvana. The Gosvāmins of Vṛndāvana (16th century C.E.) are widely regarded in the modern Caitanya tradition as the most authoritative presenters of the tradition. They are believed by many to have been taught by Caitanya himself.[4] Among the Gosvāmins, Manindranath quotes Sanātana Gosvāmin far more than the others. This is somewhat unusual, because it is usually Rūpa Gosvāmin who gets most of the attention in such scriptural discussions. This focus on Sanātana drives home the point quite nicely that Sanātana, as the eldest, was in many ways the trailblazer among the Gosvāmins. The other Gosvāmins, especially his younger brother Śrī Rūpa and his nephew Śrī Jīva, developed certain aspects of Sanātana's thought to a far greater degree than he did, but Sanātana deserves credit for pointing them in very rewarding directions. This return to Sanātana probably reflects in Manin-

[4]And so is it represented by Kṛṣṇadāsa Kavirāja (16th century CE) in his *Caitanya-caritāmṛta*.

dranath and in those practitioners of Caitanya Vaiṣṇavism in Vraja with whom he associated a renewed desire to tap into one of the most original sources of insight in the tradition, a source that even Śrī Caitanya himself appears to have relied on.[5] After Sanātana, the most quoted of the Gosvāmins in Manindranath's book is Śrī Jīva. Śrī Rūpa, though only called on occasionally, nevertheless makes several very important contributions to the discussion.

There is a good deal of repetition in Manindranath's book. This can be quite disconcerting to readers who are not used to it. Those who are used to repetition or who subscribe to a cyclical worldview, as many Caitanya Vaiṣṇavas do, will perhaps find it reassuring or even enjoyable. Manindranath seemed aware of this as a protential problem when he wrote the introduction to the second edition. He invokes there the maxim of "digging or fixing the post" (*sthūṇā-nikhanana-nyāya*), one of those numerous examples of folk wit and wisdom that are referred to in Sanskrit works by brief, pithy maxims.[6] This maxim is used to describe a method of argumentation in which an excess of evidence is supplied to make an already strong point even stronger. Just as one fixes a post securely in the ground by repeatedly pounding it in, so has Manindranath repreatedly driven home his main point, that there is no better way to develop love for Kṛṣṇa at this time or, for that matter, at any time than through *saṅkīrtana* of the names of Kṛṣṇa. For Manindranath and for the audience he targeted with this book, repetition is not a fault but a good quality. As he says in that same introduction: Repetition such as this increases the ocean of joy. Hearing such things over and over, then, is considered a source of pleasure. That is because his message is basically a positive message, a message of hope and well-being that points to a bright future. It is a gospel of love and thus is pleasing to the ears of the believers.

While Manindranath's message is basically a message of good news, there is nevertheless a trace of a sharp edge to it. Those who practice the Vaiṣṇava practice of remembrance (*smaraṇa*, a kind of meditative practice involving visualization of and projecting oneself into the daily activities of Rādhā and Kṛṣṇa in their eternal paradise) will find a sharp blade hidden in the soft gauze of Manindranath's words. In Manindranath's view one should not on one's own initiative take up that kind

[5] *Caitanya-caritāmṛta*, 3.4.155: "You are my teacher, a respected authority." Śrī Caitanya says this to Sanātana according to Kṛṣṇadāsa Kavirāja.

[6] This one is used by Śaṅkarācārya. It is found in his commentary on *Vedānta-sūtra*, 3.3.53.

of practice. To do so would be to diminish the importance of *saṅkīrtana*. Rather, remembering will grow organically out of the practice of utterance *saṅkīrtana* of the holy names when the time is right. It should not be undertaken artificially before one is ready. He uses a rather odd example to characterize the way the practice of remembering enters into the life of the practitioner. It is like being possessed by a ghost, he says. In the way that without desiring a ghost, a ghost may come and possess one and having taken one over may refuse to leave, so does remembering come uninvited and possess one and once it arrives, it never again departs. One need not strive separately for remembering. Instead, one should devote all one's effort and attention to *saṅkīrtana* of Kṛṣṇa's names and then, when the time is ripe uninterrupted remembering of Kṛṣṇa will land on one's shoulders like a ghost dropping from a tree and take possession of one's heart. Like a ghost, too, once it arrives it will not easily depart.

From Manindranath's somewhat peculiar example one should not get the idea that remembering, like being haunted by a ghost, is an unwanted experience among Caitanya Vaiṣṇavas. Constant remembering of Kṛṣṇa is in fact a sign of having arrived at the highest level of religious cultivation in Caitanya Vaiṣṇavism. Someone who deeply loves Kṛṣṇa will constantly be thinking about him and saying his name and will not forget him even for a second. This characteristic of one who has attained that perfect love for Kṛṣṇa in turn becomes one of the main forms of practice for those who are striving for that perfect love. This is an age-old principle behind religious practice in India and has been recognized as such by saint-scholars as different as and as separated in time and place as Śrī Śaṅkarācārya (7th century C.E., South India) and Śrī Sanātana Gosvāmin (16th century C.E., North India).[7] Manindranath's point here is that the path to the perfection of all-consuming love for Kṛṣṇa, which is accompanied by a constant, loving, and spontaneous remembrance of Kṛṣṇa, runs most directly through the practice of singing and repeating Kṛṣṇa's names.

Another point that Manindranath makes that is worthy of note has to do with his beliefs about Kṛṣṇa's peculiar methods of appearing to and disappearing before his devotees. Perhaps he wished to reassure those practitioners who have been at the practice a long time and were wondering why Kṛṣṇa had not appeared to them yet. Manindranath presents scriptural evidence from the works of the Gosvāmins to show

[7] See Śaṅkara on *Bhāgavad-gītā*, 2.55 and Sanātana on *Bṛhad-bhāgavatāmṛta*, 2.6.168.

that Kṛṣṇa will often appear briefly to his advanced devotees and then withdraw from them. The purpose of this withdrawal is to intensify their desire and passion for him. The classic example is, of course, his disappearance from the cowherd girls who went into the Vṛndāvana forest to meet him at night. According to the *Bhāgavata* account, Kṛṣṇa disappeared from the company of the group taking with him one special cowherd girl (Rādhā). The cowherd women who were left behind wandered about the forest in the night seeking him, inquiring about Kṛṣṇa's whereabouts from all the plants, trees, and animals they met. When he finally reappeared he explained his behavior to them in a very interesting verse:

> But, though they are worshiping me, I do not reveal myself to living beings so that their attachment, eagerness and longing for me will increase. It is just like a poor person who, after finding a great treasure, has lost it. Consumed by the thought of it, he knows nothing else.[8]

Thus, his disappearance from the cowherd girls and eventually from that one special cowherd girl, too, is meant to increase the intensity of their longing for him. This is based on the idea taken from the realm of literary criticism that love-in-separation increases the intensity and sweetness of the love enjoyed in union. Shortly after this verse in the *Purāṇa*, however, comes the famous verse in which Kṛṣṇa tells the cowherd women that he is unable to repay them for their goodness in loving him and suggests that their own goodness be their ultimate repayment.[9]

Theology of the Holy Name

About the time I rediscovered Manindranatha Babu's little book on the holy name, I also discovered that, like his book, there were sev-

---

[8]Bhāg., 10.32.20:

नाहं तु सख्यो भजतोऽपि जन्तून्
भजाम्यमीषामनुवृत्तिवृत्तये।
यथाधनो लब्धधने विनष्टे
तच्चिन्तयान्यन्निभृतो न वेद॥

[9]Bhāg. 10.32.22. There is something final and foreboding about that verse that must have suggested to Sanātana the idea of final separation that he puts forward in his *Bṛhad-bhāgavatāmṛta*, Part One, Chapter Seven.

eral other books devoted to the discussion of the holy name in Caitanya Vaiṣṇavism and written not by scholars for scholars but by practitioners for other practitioners. Though not the product of critical scholarship, the books were nevertheless scholarly in their own fashion, containing discussions of and numerous references to works considered authoritative in the Caitanya tradition. This area of thought and writing I have come to refer to as the theology of the holy name.

The practices of reciting the names of Kṛṣṇa, meditating on them, and singing them loudly with musical accompaniment have been a prominent feature of Caitanya Vaiṣṇavism from its very beginning. Most Caitanya Vaiṣṇavas recognize repetition of the holy names as the foundation upon which the entire religious tradition was built. As a result, a great deal of thought and discussion has been devoted, especially in the late 19th and early 20th centuries, to the names of Kṛṣṇa, their relationship to Kṛṣṇa, the one who is named, and their efficacy in bringing about what is regarded as purification of the minds and hearts of the tradition's practitioners. The ultimate goal of all the practices of the Caitanya tradition is to cultivate an intense and deeply emotional love for Kṛṣṇa, a love that overpowers and subdues all other loves and brings those loves into alignment with itself. The primary driving force behind this cultivation is the divine power believed to be invested in the names of Kṛṣṇa.

There is a great deal of that old, primitive, magical thinking connected with names and naming in this Caitanyaite system of beliefs concerning the names of Kṛṣṇa. It was a commonly held belief in ancient and primitive societies that by knowing the name of something one gains control or power over it. The name is somehow intimately connected with or inseparable from the person or thing named. Thus, names were often kept secret as one sees for instance in the way the name of God (YHWH) was handled in the Hebrew Bible. It was never pronounced because it bears the awful and dangerous power of the one who is named, God himself. By uttering the name of God one was placing oneself in God's powerful presence, too close for comfort, which, considering how God was conceived in the Hebrew Bible, was considered a definite threat to one's health.

One can see a similar way of thinking in the ancient hymns of the Vedas. There the names of the gods are used along with various praises to invoke them and make them present at the rituals at which the hymns were sung. Thus, the names are used there to bring the gods close so that an interaction with them (offerings and requests) can more easily be made. It was not so much a matter of calling the gods as it was of making them present by the very pronunciation of their names. The names were the gods and the gods their names. Knowing the correct names of the gods and pronouncing them correctly was considered the difference between a successful and an unsuccessful rite. Thus, the power of the rites was in the *brahman*, the sacred speech and especially in the sacred names. Those who spoke the sacred speech and handled the sacred names, filled with sacred power (*brahman*), were known as the *brāhmaṇas*, the ritual specialists.

A similar principle operates even in the Upaniṣads, the later and final portions of the Vedas. There certain words, the great statements (*mahāvākya*), for instance, were believed to have great power and efficacy. Thus, when the famous Upaniṣadic statement *tattvamasi*, "you are that (*brahman*, here spirit or self)," was pronounced by the Upaniṣadic teacher at the conclusion of his teaching to his dear disciples, the ignorance (*avidyā*) of the student was supposed to be overcome suddenly by the light of knowledge and realizing himself to be *brahman*, the student would respond with *ahaṁ brahmāsmi*, "I am *brahman*." The words are the things they represent. There was, it was believed, a unity between word (*pada*) and meaning (*artha*). Thus the Vedas and the Upaniṣads were restricted to the hearing of only certain groups and that only after ritual initiation.

On this ancient background, the fundamental principles of the theology of the holy name developed: That the name and the named are not different, are inseparable. To use an example drawn from Manindranath's book: They are the same sweet, candy syrup poured into two different molds, one a syllabic form and the other a human-like form. Of course, a radical distinction is drawn between mundane names and the names of Kṛṣṇa (including the names of his various descents and expansions). Mundane names *are* different from the things or persons they name. That is why one can say "pie" and not have one's mouth filled with pie. But, the case is different with Kṛṣṇa, the holy name theologians tell us. Utter his name and he is fully there, personally present on one's tongue and in one's ears and in the ears of all those who hear his name at that instant. His presence brings about an immediate transformation in one if one is without offense when one says or hears Kṛṣṇa's name, or a gradual purification of the senses and mind if one is not. The chanter eventually becomes able to see into and experience the otherwise invisible spiritual realm of Kṛṣṇa.

Therefore, to the fundamental doctrine of the unity of holy name and the holy named, are added some discussions of the various obstacles that interfere with the efficacy of the holy name: The offenses (*aparādha*). Then, one can add some discussion of the borderline cases called "semblance or similitude of the holy name" (*nāmābhāsa*) in which the holy name is applied to someone who is not the holy named. When one adds some discussion of the relationship between chanting the holy names and other forms of *bhakti* practice (hearing discourses on sacred topics, worship of images, meditation, pilgrimage and so forth), one has all the main elements of that area of thought in Caitanya Vaiṣṇavism called the theology of the holy name.

One often also finds in the theology of the holy name glorification of the powers of the holy name to destroy sins, to save or free one from rebirth and discussions involving the peculiar cyclic view of time commonly found in Hinduism. In that system it is claimed that we are currently living in the fourth or worst of all ages, the Age of One or the Age of Quarrel (Kali-yuga), and that therefore all other forms of spiritual cultivation, being more complicated and difficult to perform, are beyond our reach. Only the chanting of the holy names, especially when it is done loudly, in a group, and with musical accompaniment, can save us in this dark, diminished age. This came to be regarded in the tradition as the one great quality of this age, that the highest form of the divine love can be approached so easily through the repetition of the divine names and approached by everyone no matter what their qualifications might be.

Other Works on the Theology of the Holy Names

There are several outstanding figures in the more recent history of the Caitanya Vaiṣṇava tradition who have written on the theology of the holy names. They are theologians of the holy names because of their efforts to try to flesh out that special domain of Caitanya Vaiṣṇava theology. Perhaps the earliest of them was Vipinavihārī Gosvāmin whose work entitled the *Hari-nāmāmṛta-sindhu* (Ocean of the Nectar of Hari's Names) was completed in 1878.[10] It has twelve chapters called *taraṅga* (waves) and is written in Bengali verse with Sanskrit verses interspersed.

[10]It was apparently published in 1879. There is a copy of the 1879 edition in the British Library (shelf-mark VT1850).

The chapters of Vipinavihārī's book are entitled: (1) The *dharma*[11] of the age and the good quality of the Age of Kali, (2) The greatness of the names of Hari, (3) The method of glorifying Hari and the greatness of such glorification, (4) The method of hearing the names of Hari and the greatness of that hearing, (5) The method of remembering the names of Hari and the greatness of that remembering, (6) The method of thinking of Hari and the greatness of that thinking, (7) Description of the origination of the names of Hari, (8) Inquiry into Śrī Rādhā, (9) Description of Hari and Brahman and the real difference between them, (10) The practice of cultivating the names of Hari, (11) Description of the way of attaining *bhakti*[12] for Hari, and (12) Description of the different kinds of *bhakti* for Hari. He draws together hundreds of Sanskrit verses from a variety of sources, organizes them into those twelve general headings and provides his own translation-commentary on them in versified Bengali. As one can tell from the titles of the chapters, much more is covered here than just the holy names. The practice of reciting the names of Kṛṣṇa is used as the frame around which the system of Caitanya Vaiṣṇava beliefs is organized. The same might be said of this book of Manindranath's. Much more than the holy names is covered in connection with his discussion.

One of Vipinavihārī Gosvāmin's major disciples was Ṭhākura Bhaktivinoda (1838-1914). He wrote, among numerous other works on Caitanya Vaiṣṇavism, a classic work on the theology of the holy names called the *Śrī Hari-nāma-cintāmaṇi* (Thought-jewel of the Names of Hari). It is also written in Bengali verse, though here no Sanskrit verses are interspersed. It is written in the form of a dialogue between Śrī Caitanya and Haridāsa, a Muslim who became a follower of Śrī Caitanya and who is recognized in the old biographies of Caitanya as the "Teacher of the Holy Name" (*nāmācārya*). According to Bhaktivinoda's text, Śrī Caitanya after finishing his bath in the ocean at Purī comes one day to the Bakula tree under which he and his followers often used to meet. There he asks Haridāsa what the easiest way for living beings to find salvation is. Haridāsa reviews all the various options and concludes that "remembering the holy names and *saṅkīrtana* of the holy names is all the living beings need to observe."[13] The dialogue continues on from there

---

[11]The recommended religious practice. See the glossary for a more detailed discussion of the semantic range of the word *dharma* in Indic religion.

[12]See the glossary.

[13]Bhaktivinoda Ṭhākura, *Śrī Harināmacintāmaṇi*, p. 14. (Nadia (West Bengal): Jagajjīvanadāsa, 1963) I do not have a date for the original publication of the text. It was

in a very systematic and organized manner. There are fifteen chapters in the book. The first three are entitled: "Indications of the Greatness of the Holy Names," "Considerations about Reciting the Holy Names," and "Considerations about Semblance of the Holy Names (*nāmābhāsa*). Chapters Four through Thirteen are each about one of the ten offenses to the holy name. Chapter Fourteen is about offenses in the matter of service and Chapter Fifteen is about the method of worship by means of the holy names. This last chapter discusses the various stages in the process of rising to the peak experience of *rasa* or sacred rapture through the chanting of the holy names. With Bhaktivinoda's book the theology of the holy names began to take on its characteristic shape, involving a discussion of the offenses, of the non-difference posited between the holy names and the holy named, and of the superiority of the practice of reciting the names to other forms of *bhakti*.

In the 20th century there were a number of writers on the holy names. Perhaps the greatest of them was Manindranath's guru Kanupriya Goswami. His work, which eventually extended to three volumes, is entitled the *Śrī Śrī Nāma-cintāmaṇi* (Thought-jewel of the Holy Name). Because of his work on the Holy Names Kanupriya Goswami was recognized in the Vaiṣṇava community as the "Teacher of the Science of the Holy Names" (*nāma-vijñānācārya*). The first volume of Kanupriya Goswami's book (1943) is on the nature and fundamental principles of the holy name. It contains eight chapters and they are entitled: (1) The necessity and superiority of scriptural evidence, (2) The name and the named, (3) The power and the possessor of power, (4) The non-difference of the Lord and His name, (5) The distinctiveness of the holy name in the definition of the name and the semblance of the name, (6) The true nature of the Lord and the non-difference of the name from that true nature, (7) The non-difference of the form of the Lord from His true nature, and (8) The superiority of the name of the Lord over the Lord's true nature and form. Volume Two (1979) gives a detailed and subtle discussion of the ten offenses to the holy name with numerous quotes from the scriptural sources. The introduction contains what is described as a history of the offenses to the holy names. Volume Three of Kanupriya's book (1989) is a long and involved commentary on the first verse of the eight verses of instruction attributed to Śrī Caitanya. There he develops in great detail the idea that the whole process of *bhakti* cultivation, from the beginning of practice to the experience of the higher stages of *preman*, is described in the progressively ordered parts of that one verse.

certainly first published after Vipinavihārī's work in 1879, however.

Manindranath gives a very abbreviated version of discussion towards the end of this book as well.

Inspired by Kanupriya's work another great scholar of the modern Vaiṣṇava tradition, Sundarānanda Vidyāvinoda, wrote a work in Bengali on the theology of the holy names called *Śrī Śrī Nāma-cintāmaṇi-kiraṇa-kaṇikā* (A Small Ray of Light from the Thought-jewel of the Holy Names) spanning nearly six hundred pages. His work is primarily an extended commentary on Śrī Rūpa Gosvāmin's eight verses on the names of Kṛṣṇa called the "Eight on Kṛṣṇa's Names" (*Kṛṣṇa-nāmāṣṭaka*). It contains eighteen chapters covering all the major topics of the theology of the holy name already mentioned with copious citations from the original Sanskrit and Bengali texts. It also contains an appendix that contains all the names of Kṛṣṇa that are mentioned in the *Bhāgavata Purāṇa* with glosses on their meanings from the commentaries of the major Caitanyaite commentators. In short, it is a massive work by one of the best writers in the Caitanya tradition in the 20th century.

Manindranath Guha's book is thus only the most recent work in a long line of works on the theology of the holy name stretching back almost a century and it is probably the shortest among them. It nevertheless manages to raise all the questions that are considered important in this area of Caitanyaite thought and the answers one finds in it are not always what one would expect. Manindranath was certainly aware of many of the works written before on the subject, especially those by his teacher. He was probably also familiar with the work by Bhaktivinoda Ṭhākura and by Sundarānanda Vidyāvinoda. Manindranath's book is thus a fine introduction to this wealth of Vaiṣṇava theological reflection on the nature of the holy name that has occupied some of the modern tradition's finest thinkers and writers.

The Translation

This translation has been done with two audiences in mind. The first consists of scholars and students of world religions who would benefit from reading an accessible and relatively short religious tract on the essential practices and beliefs of Caitanya Vaiṣṇavism written by a Caitanya Vaiṣṇava for other Caitanya Vaiṣṇavas. I have kept that audience in mind in providing a good deal of explanatory and scholarly apparatii in the form of introduction, footnotes (clearly identified as my own), glossaries, and bibliography. I think the members of this audience will learn a great deal about this tradition from this little book. Almost all of the fundamental beliefs and practices of the tradition are clearly if only briefly discussed. Such readers will find much that is familiar in the work, much that reminds them of certain segments of their own traditions, no doubt, or of other traditions with which they are familiar. The text is thoroughly theistic. One feels that in some places one could almost replace Kṛṣṇa and Rādhā with Yahweh, Jesus, or Allah and transform the work into a fine Jewish, Christian, or Muslim text. The insistence that "there is no other way" with respect to *saṅkīrtana* of the holy names is reminiscent of Christianity's insistence on its having cornered the market on truth in Jesus. The focus on God's names recalls both Jewish (Kabbalah) and Islamic mysticism (Sufism). The convoluted, hair-splitting, and subtle lengths to which Manindranath sometimes must go, guided no doubt by his Gosvāmin teachers, to interpret "properly" a troublesome verse of scripture is common in almost all religious traditions with highly developed literatures.

For members of the Caitanya tradition I have done my best to translate Manindranath's work faithfully so that they might reap the benefits he hoped that they would from it. All of his footnotes, which he primarily uses to cite passages of Sanskrit in support of the points he makes, are present and have been checked and corrected whenever necessary. I have capitalized words the way I think he would have wanted (Lord instead of lord, Holy Name instead of holy name). I have avoided, however, the overly saccharine kind of language that is usually found in English works belonging to the Caitanya tradition.

My translation has attempted to stay as close as possible to Manindranath's original Bengali text while yet translating it into idiomatically correct English. This has not been too hard to do and I have sometimes wondered to myself if Manindranath, who knew English quite well, did not have an English form of expression in mind when he wrote certain passages. At times it simply seemed too easy to come up with an English expression comparable to Manindranath's Bengali wording. There were some passages, though, in which it was difficult to find a suitable English expression for Manindranath's Bengali. In those places I have done the best I could with my understanding of his intended sense and have called attention to them in my footnotes.

As mentioned before, this translation is based on the second revised edition. No later edition of it was produced out as far as I know. Manindranath has not written in the high literary style called *sādhu-bhāṣa*. Most of the other works on the theology of the holy name mentioned above are written in the high literary style. Instead, Manindranath chose the more common colloquial style called *calita*. Why he chose this style is not clear, but perhaps he felt that the colloquial form of the language was more appropriate for the book's structure as a dialogue. The literary form of Bengali used in ordinary speech must sound as stilted as Shakespearean English might to the modern English speaker. That said, it must be noted that the vocabulary is decidedly Sanskritic. The Persian, Arabic, and Portuguese borrowings that are so common in colloquial Bengali appear to have been bleached out of Manindranath's language.

I was faced with a tough choice when Manindranath translates a Sanskrit verse into Bengali. I could have translated the Sanskrit directly from the Sanskrit or from the Bengali of Manindranath's translation. I chose the latter because sometimes Manindranath adds things to or emphasizes things in his Bengali translations that are not obvious in the Sanskrit. Not to translate those verses in the way Manindranath did would have interfered with the flow of his argument. When this sort of thing happens in the translation I have noted in a footnote the difference between what the Sanskrit actually says and what Manindranath says it says. Fortunately, this does not happen often because, in general, Manindranath's translations are faithful to the original. Occasionally, however, his enthusiasm or desire to make a particular point seems to carry him away, and he puts words into the mouths of those he translates. For instance, when Sanātana says something like "the highest good" (*parama-śubha*), Manindranath says "the loving service of Rādhā." This is certainly what Manindranath thinks the highest good is, but is it necessarily what Sanātana thinks, too? Manindranath's interpretation of his words in that way imposes his own notion of the highest good on Sanātana's.

Some Sanskrit-Bengali words simply have no satisfying equivalents in English. Such words I have left in the original and given a more detailed account of their meanings in the glossary. Perhaps the most important example of this sort of word are *saṅkīrtana* and its close relative *kīrtana*. I tried several English possibilities for this word at various points during the translation: praising, glorifying, reciting, repeating, etc. Its meaning incorporates all of those possibilities and I found I was not satisfied with any one of them individually. Their connection with the word *kīrti*, which means "fame," suggests that it has to do with making someone famous or spreading the fame of someone or some thing. *Saṅkīrtana* of the holy name, however, does not mean, except perhaps in a secondary way, spreading the fame of the holy name. It means spreading the fame of the holy named *by means* of the holy names. Taken as repeating or reciting, it means the rite of reciting the holy names. *Saṅkīrtana* can be connected also with Kṛṣṇa's forms, qualities, and actions. In each case it means praising Kṛṣṇa by speaking about his forms, qualities, and actions. None of the English words I tried seemed to convey all of this well. So I left it in its original Sanskrit form. There are a few other words like this, too, words such as *dharma* and *bhakti*. Detailed discussions of those words can be found in the glossary at the back of the book.

In closing, I would like to say that it has been a pleasure for me over the past few years to try to think along with Manindranath on this topic so dear to the hearts of Caitanya Vaiṣṇavas. I hope that the members of the two audiences to which I aimed this translation will have an equally good time following its winding, unhurried progression through the exotic, richly forested, flower-filled world of Caitanya Vaiṣṇavism.

Blessings

Manindranath Guha's Dīkṣā Guru

Śrī Kanupriya Goswami

(From a letter written to the author dated 1-5-1970)[14]

In reviewing your book (*Śrī Mādhava-mādhurya-mañjuṣā, Treasure Chest of the Sweetness of Mādhava [Kṛṣṇa]*),[15] that which has been given by the great, realized Vaiṣṇavas saints of Vṛndāvana is a source of joy. Even though the book is your first effort, the way it has achieved such high critical praise means that the path for your writing of future books will remain auspicious and open. This is indeed sufficiently hopeful. Whatever happens, together with performing *saṅkīrtana* of the Holy Names, the writing of your books and the performing of your own worship (*bhajana*) — this will make your life sweet like a shower in the sacred waters of the Triveṇī.[16] Thus, your residence in the holy land[17] will be fruitful. This is my hope for you.

[14]Though this letter does not refer specifically to the book translated here (the *Nectar of the Holy Name*), it constitutes in Mani Babu's eyes a blessing given to him by his guru on all his future works. This letter was written after the publication of Mani Babu's first book. I believe his guru had passed away before Manindranath's book on the Holy Name was published.

[15]Manindranath Babu's first book, published in 1969.

[16]The confluence of the three main sacred rivers in India: the Gaṅgā, the Yamunā, and the Sarasvatī. They join together at Allahabad and a bath in that confluence is considered extremely sanctifying.

[17]Vṛndāvana

Manindranath Guha's Śikṣā Guru

Śrī Kiśorīkiśorānanda Bābā (Tin Kuḍi Goswami)

Hearing before that the spotless, full moon had set in India's sky of good fortune[18] I was deeply pained inside. After getting your letter and understanding the details of it contents I felt some hope and some peace. Even though he has disappeared, the power of his *bhakti* for the Lord, endowed with his soothing and brilliant moonlight, has been established in you. This is indeed our good fortune. In the *bhakti* scriptures you have translated, the inward feelings of the Goswami are manifested. This sort of unprecedentedly wonderful narration is not possible for an ordinary living being. By the limitless grace your guru placed on you Śrīman Mahāprabhu sits inside you and narrates.

First one has [in your books] the truth of Śrī Gaura and Govinda's forms, qualities and sports and on top of that they are narrated through the lips of a devotee. Hearing the *Śrī Caitanya-candrodaya Nāṭaka* from your lips has filled even a worldly-minded person like me with joy.

May Śrī Śrī Rādhāvallabha bestow happiness upon you. Offering a *tulasi* leaf dipped in sandalwood to the feet of Śrī Śrī Rādhāvallabha, I pray that you will be healthy and long-lived, that while relishing the *bhakti-rasa* of the Lord you may bring about our good fortune and that of India as well.

[18] This is a reference to the then recent passing of Manindranath Babu's *dīkṣā* guru, Śrī Kanupriya Goswami.

Introduction

For those of us who think of ourselves as members of the community (*sampradāya*) started by Śrī Gaurahari, the time has indeed come for us to contemplate deeply on where we have arrived after having wandered step by step, under the influence of time, from the path that was started by him. If this self examination is to be carried out, we have to enter with open minds into the collection of books that the Gosvāmins left behind for us. If today we do not carry out this self-examination those whom we refer to as the heretical community (*apasampradāya*) will come and snatch away by force our rightful inheritance. We will no longer be able to find a way into it. If we are to become strong in our own fortress, we will need to take hold of the tremendously potent words of the Gosvāmins. Our power is deposited in them. Whatever we have heard, whatever we have understood, we will have to reconcile that with the words of the Gosvāmins.

In this *Drop from the Ocean of Nectar* the fundamental teaching of the path and philosophy founded by Śrī Gaura has been firmly established through the writings of the Gosvāmins. Beneath each statement citations from words of the Gosvāmins have been given in the footnotes. The fundamental teaching can be known from his (Śrī Gaura's) name — he is called the "father of *saṅkīrtana*." *Saṅkīrtana* is the creation of Lord Śrī Kṛṣṇa Caitanya.[19]

The way a father is extremely devoted to his son, that is the way Śrī Gaurahari feels towards this *saṅkīrtana*. He intensely identifies with it. Among all the kinds of offerings that are used in the worship of Śrī Gaurahari, who is this age's chief object of worship, *saṅkīrtana* is the best.

---

[19]Kavi Karṇapūra, Ccn., 8.42: इयमियं भगवत्कृष्णचैतन्यसृष्टिः ।

In it his satisfaction is the greatest. It is not only that it is the best of all — it is essential.

If one is able to go around loudly singing and dancing in the *saṅkīrtana* of the Holy Names that Gaura created like someone half mad, then even without remembering and the other forms of *bhakti* cultivation one can enter into the bowers of Vraja. On the other hand, without resorting to the most essential of practices, that is, *saṅkīrtana* of the Holy Names, the path to success by the other forms of practice becomes indeed very difficult to negotiate. This principle has been very clearly expressed in this book on the basis of the evidence of the Gosvāmins' writings.

By expert choice of words and cleverness of composition the subject matter has been very beautifully expressed in this book. Mr. Guha has given us sufficient introduction to his expertise in writing, his powers of perception, and his erudition by writing and editing many works on *bhakti* previously. I believe that like his previous books this book too will be properly acclaimed in the society of Vaiṣṇavas. Those who regard the words of the Gosvāmins as one of their treasures will feel immense pleasure in reading this book and will be greatly benefitted. This book will act as a lantern for the practitioner on the path of worship. I desire to spread the news of this book greatly. The author is a dear object of my affection and making known to him my blessings, I end my comments.

Jaya Śrī Nitāi Gaura

Śrī Gaurāṅga Dāsa Bābāji Mahārāja
President of the Gauḍeśvara Vaiṣṇava Sammilanī
Former Mahanta of Rādhākuṇḍa

The Author's (Laghu's) Dedication

Like a hunchback's desire to lie down on his back this low-born, illiterate, a hundred times offensive householder's desire to discuss scripture is laughable. This is arrogance indeed. Still, who knows? Behind me there is a planet, mischievous or good-natured I don't know which, that makes me dance about — it gives me no opportunity to consider my qualification or lack thereof.

There is one more consideration. In just the same way that Kāj-pāglā was saved by finally giving that demon the job of going up and down the bamboo stick,[20] this writing of books of mine has arisen as a matter of course in order to save myself — otherwise what would I do with my wandering and mischievous mind? Wandering off to some bad or unsuitable places it would wind up finally destroying me.

The scriptures are revealed from the Lord who is the very embodiment of scripture. Those who bind that Lord in the temples of their hearts with the ropes of love are able to become commentators on scripture. Modern folks like me are only able to distribute those commentaries among the populace — whatever little bit is possible.

I have tried to distribute a single drop of nectar in this little book. Not one statement here is my own — it is from my teachers. Of all that Śrī Gaurahari and his followers have said, the basis of this book is whatever tiny drop of that nectar, issuing from the lotus-like lips of my teachers, that has fallen on my mind. My reflection on that drop

[20] I am unfamiliar with this story. [Trans.]

is this *Drop of the Ocean.*[21] This is an other-worldly thing. It will not become corrupted by the touch of my wicked mind. This is my belief. May you Vaiṣṇavas, who are by nature not finders-of-fault, correct the mistakes and failings of my words — and please don't forget to show this low, unfortunate person a little mercy. I have come to you with the desire of being sprinkled with the dust of your feet. I beg you. Don't be stingy; show me your mercy. The days of this lowlife, racked by the offense of conceit, are coming to an end. Don't let me die just carrying about loads of sugar like a sugar-ox.[22] Let me have the good fortune of tasting a little, too.

When my teacher gave me his blessings for my edition and translation of the *Caitanya-candrodaya-nāṭaka*, he said: "May he be able to remain dedicated to these kinds of great undertakings — may Śrī Gaurahari always spread his grace on them." Holding my teacher's blessing on my head, I placed this "drop from the ocean" in the hands of my publisher.[23]

Jaya Śrī Nāmaprabhu!

An impersonator of a servant
of the servants of the Vaiṣṇavas,
Manindranath Guha (Laghu)
Goṣṭhāṣṭamī,
24 Kārtika, 1382 [1976]

---

[21] "A Drop of the Ocean of the Nectar of the Holy Name" is the literal translation of Mani Babu's Bengali title for this book. That has been shortened to *Nectar of the Holy Name* in this translation.

[22] *Cinir balada*, a Bengali expression for someone who works hard for someone else's profit but cannot share it.

[23] Mani Babu's publisher was his wife, Savitri Guha, who had an MA in Sanskrit and two Tīrthas, one in Purāṇas and one in Vaiṣṇava philosophy. A *tīrtha*, holy ford, that is, a place where a difficult-to-cross river may be crossed, is a special degree given for advanced study in a particular subject in the native system of Sanskrit education in India.

Appreciations

Expert in Private Worship, Great Scholar,
Adorned by the *Bhāgavata*, and
Resident of Govardhana,

Śrī Priyācaraṇa Dāsa Bābā

Though but a drop of the Holy Names,
yet like an ocean in depth,
Victory to this the beautiful
Nectar of Hari's Holy Names,
a benefit to the whole world.[24]

Reading the book, *A Drop of the Ocean of the Nectar of the Holy Names*, by Manindranath Guha, I felt immense joy. Though the book is called "a drop" it is more like an ocean. In the life of a Gauḍīya Vaiṣṇava practitioner, all the questions that generally arise have been accurately answered with great skill. That skill is revealed in different ways. Śrī Gaurahari speaking to Rāma Rāya has said to the world: "Recite a verse that describes the highest objective." That order has been followed in every statement of this book. Seeing this marshalling of appropriate citations one must conclude that Mr. Guha has entered deeply into the depths of the ocean of scripture like a seasoned diver. His ability to consider what is prior and what is subsequent is fully mature. The subtlety of his arguments is irrefutable. I am able to say with certainty that Gauḍīya

[24]Composed by Priyācaraṇa Dāsa Bābā:

नाम्नां बिन्दुस्तथाप्येष गाम्भीर्यें सिन्धुसन्निभः।
नामामृतं हरेः श्रीमज्जयति विश्वमङ्गलम्॥

Vaiṣṇava practitioners will be greatly helped by reading this book. I desire that this book, which bears within it the sweetness of the glory of the Holy Name, the very life source of our community, be spread far and wide.

Mr. Guha is one of my own, a very dear object of my affection. May he live a long life and be engaged in the service of our community by writing and editing many more books like this one. This is my prayer at Śrī Gaura's feet.

An insignificant servant
of the servants of the Vaiṣṇavas,
Śrī Priyācaraṇa Dāsa Bābā

Established in renunciation, knowledge, and *bhakti*,
Great Scholar, and resident of Vṛndāvana

Amar Sen

I received your book, *Drop of the Ocean of Nectar of the Holy Names,* from Śāstrī. I read it with great enthusiasm and offer my humble obeisances at your feet over and over. Taking shelter in the Holy Names is our main form of practice. You have taken all of the problems that arise in the heart of the practitioner while he or she is cultivating the Holy Names and put them in question form. Then you have given all of the solutions to those problems in an unprecedented way, citing all the scriptural evidence. Thus you have given a great gift to the world of practitioners like us. Those of us practitioners who follow the Vaiṣṇava view will remain eternally grateful to you.

An insignigicant servant
of the servants of the Vaiṣṇavas,
Śrī Amar Sen

Dedication of the Second Edition

Though there is no good arrangement for its distribution, by Śrī Gaurahari's grace the first edition of this book is nearly gone. Since the demand for it is increasing more and more, it is necessary to bring out this second edition. Such a rapid exhaustion of an edition of a book on religion is undoubtedly a very encouraging sign for an author. This second edition has grown a good deal in size. Like a flowing river, it runs bubbling along amidst the addition of new topics and the expanded discussion of the older topics as needed. The Name and offense to the Name are the measures of our life and death. On this topic, like in the maxim of fixing in the post[25] repeating again and again is required — as much as it is repeated, that much is the ocean of joy increased — here there is no such thing as too much.

Śrī Jīva in the beginning of his *Harināmāmṛta-vyākaraṇa* (Grammar of the Ambrosia of the Names of Hari) has said:

> "Shortening by even half a syllable is as joyous as the birth of a son;" this is the statement of the [Sanskrit] grammarians. In the case of the syllables of the name of Hari, however, that sort of reasoning is condemned.[26]

[25] "As a stake or post to be firmly fixed in the ground is again and again moved and thrust inward, so this maxim is used when one (say, a disputant) adds several corroborative illustrations, arguments, etc. to strengthen and confirm still more firmly his strong position." Apte, *Sanskrit-English Dictionary*, Appendix E, p. 76.

[26] Hnv, 1.2:

मात्रालाघवमात्रं पुत्रोत्सव इति परेऽभिमन्यन्ते। हरिनामलाभाद्वयं त्वमूदृक् तिरस्कुर्मः॥

This book's main purpose is to sing the glories of Lord Holy Name (Nāmaprabhu) and after seating him in his proper place, on the throne of the emperor, to carry out his worship. There is no intention in this of putting down any other form of worship. Whatever has been placed wherever in a comparative manner, that is all done on the strength of the path approved by all the saints and the scriptures. "Then Sūta Gosāi in his heart felt great fear. Whatever was the characteristic of something, that he ascertained."[27]

> When Śrī Gaurahari, whose complexion was like molten gold, was before the eyes of the world, the universe was submerged in the flavors of love and the practice of loud, tumultuous *kīrtana* of Hari was started. Alas! Will that sweet time ever return again?[28]

Though gradually diminishing, the heat of a lighted fire is felt for a long time. Therefore, Kṛṣṇadāsa Kavirāja, eighty-two years after the disappearance of Śrī Gaurahari, sitting on the bank of Rādhākuṇḍa wrote: "All the circles [groups] of Vaiṣṇavas who live in Vṛndāvana are fully sheltered in Kṛṣṇa's Name, most auspicious."[29] Through this verse it is understood that even eighty-two years after the disappearance of Śrī Gaurahari for all of the Vaiṣṇavas that were in Vṛndāvana the Name of Kṛṣṇa was the best of all refuges — their highest regard was for the Holy Name.

We have come a great distance since those days. The heat of that fire of love is today almost unfelt. Sarasvatī's aforementioned heartfelt

---

[27] Cc, 1.2.56:

tabe sūta gosāi mane pāñā baḍo bhaya
yār ye lakṣaṇa tāhā karila niścaya

[28] Prabodhānanda Sarasvatī, Cca, 139:

अभिव्यक्तो यत्र द्रुतकनकगौरहरिरभू-
न्महिम्न तस्यैव प्रणयरसमग्नं जगदभूत्।
अभूदुच्चैरुच्चैस्तुमुलहरिसङ्कीर्तनविधिः
स कालः किं भूयोऽप्यहह परिवर्त्तेत मधुरः॥

[29] Cc., 1.5.228:

vṛndāvane baise yata vaiṣṇava maṇḍal
kṛṣṇanāmaparāyaṇa parama maṅgal

prayer[30] is directed at living beings like us suffering in the Age of Kali. Alas, today we don't know how or when or even where the priceless gem given by our father has been lost. Today that loud, tumultuous *saṅkīrtana* of Hari is no longer heard in every house and those intense tears, shivers and goose-bumps are no longer seen in every body.[31] Nevertheless a heartfelt prayer by one of Śrī Gaura's companions cannot be unsuccessful. Those good days will again return. When will we again go out dancing in the midst of loud, tumultuous *saṅkīrtana* of Hari? When will we put aside politeness and dive into that intoxication?

O Vaiṣṇavas! Oceans of causeless mercy! Show your grace to this low, fallen person. I am only the distributor. In the confectioner's house are my lord Śrī Gaurahari and his companions. Don't cheat yourselves out of tasting *rasa* by staring at this ill-shapen distributor and wincing. Keep your gaze in the direction of the confectioners and taste this little drop. This little drop will, by the good qualities of your enriched hearts, appear like an ocean. Jaya Rādhe!

An impersonator of a servant
of the servants of the Vaiṣṇava,
Śrī Manindranatha Guha
15, Baiśakh, 1390 [1984]

---

[30] Prabodhānanda Sarasvatī, the author of the *Caitanya-candrāmṛta*, the source of the last Sanskrit verse cited above.

[31] Prabodhānada Sarasvatī, Cca, 114: अभून्नेहे गेहे तुमुलहरिसङ्कीर्तनरवो बभौ देहे देहे विपुलाश्रुव्यतिकरः

Prologue

I praise the supreme controller,
Śrī Kṛṣṇacaitanya, whose grace
makes the lame cross over mountains
and the dumb recite the Vedas.[32]

Laghu: Master, Dearest of Mukunda,[33] Teacher of the Holy Name! Today, seeing the frightening progression of this material world, my mind is depressed. Nowadays I am severely wounded by onslaughts of desires and subconscious urges. In front of me death spreads wide its mouth. In the currents of the river of time we are like little bubbles that appear for a second and then dissolve forever. In the midst of all this, what is the best and easiest way to gain victory over death and attain immortality? Please show me your grace and tell me.

Goswami: Look, the material world is like a forest fire, but until the mind is a little purified it does not notice the heat. It is a very good sign indeed that you are able to perceive it a little. Whatever the case may be, your question is very timely and appropriate. A sign of the intelligence of the intelligent and the wisdom of the wise is found in their gaining immortality by means of the mortal body.

---

[32] An oft used *maṅgala* verse:

पङ्गुं लङ्घयते शैलं मूकमावर्तयेत् श्रुतिं ।
यत्कृपा तमहं वन्दे कृष्णचैतन्यमीश्वरम् ॥

[33] One of the many names of Kṛṣṇa. It is said to be a combination of the word *muku* (liberation) and the suffix *da* (giver) meaning thus "Giver of Liberation." (Trans.)

Chapter 1

The Best Way of All

Goswami: All right then, listen. Different religious prescriptions are found in the scriptures according to person, time and place. In the peaceful Satya-yuga (Age of Truth), when the religious mind was strong, there was the prescription of meditation (*dhyāna*). Like that, in this tumultuous Age of Kali (*kali-yuga*, Age of Quarrel), when the irreligious mind is strong, *saṅkīrtana* (loud, congregational chanting)[1] of the Holy Names is the prescribed practice. When society is troubled by the flames of the three miseries,[2] when even the smallest sign of peace is not found anywhere, when society is fidgeting about in the heat of the conflagration of the sense objects produced by absorption in unnatural enjoyments, a prescription is needed that is capable of putting out that fire and granting great peace. That is why the most compassionate Lord himself, Śrī

[1] *Saṅkīrtana* has no exact or easy translation in English. It is from the Sanskrit root $\sqrt{k\bar{\imath}rt}$ which means: mention, make mention of, tell, name, call, recite, repeat, relate, declare, communicate, commemorate, celebrate, praise and glorify. Adding the *sam* prefix to the root to make the derivative noun *saṅkīrtana* gives the meaning "to celebrate completely." In the context of the Caitanya tradition this means congregational singing, often with musical accompaniment, of the names of Kṛṣṇa or of songs about him and his companions. Since this is more or less a technical term with no exact English equivalent, it is left in the text untranslated. See the glossary for a more detailed discussion of the term. (Trans.)

[2] The three miseries refers to the three sources of suffering identified in Indic traditions: sufferings caused by other living beings (*ādhibhautika*, ie. insects, animals, humans, etc), sufferings caused by one's own body or mind (*ādhyātmika*, ie. disease, old age, etc), and sufferings caused by higher powers (*ādhidaivika*, ie. natural calamaties and so forth). (Trans.)

Gaurahari,[3] came down from Goloka[4] to earth in the middle of this frenzied dance of the Age of Kali. He brought with him a downpour of the highest nectar in the form of the *saṅkīrtana* of the Holy Names, the best and most powerful means in his treasury of putting out the forest fire of material existence. He calls out to the living being burned by the three flames of Kali:

> The *saṅkīrtana* of the Names of Kṛṣṇa cleans the mirror of the mind, puts out the forest fire of the ills of material existence, acts like the moon in causing the lily of the most auspicious love for Kṛṣṇa to blossom, becomes the very life of the *bhakti* of love,[5] increases the ocean of joy, gives one tastes of the fullest nectar at every step, and floods all the senses with joy; may it gain the highest victory.[6]

He also says:

> Among the forms of worship,
> *bhakti*'s nine are best.[7]
> Love for Kṛṣṇa has great power

---

[3]Golden Hari (Viṣṇu), another name for Śrī Kṛṣṇa Caitanya. (Trans.)

[4]The eternal residence of Rādhā and Kṛṣṇa and their joined form Śrī Kṛṣṇa Caitanya. (Trans.)

[5]The original has "life of true knowledge which is like a wife" (*vidyā-vadhūjīvana*). The author, Manindranath, has translated wife-like true knowledge as the *bhakti* of love (*preman*). *Bhakti* is the attitude of fundamental secondariness towards and participation in the deity that this tradition recognizes as paramount in religious consciousness. Like the word religion which means to re-bind to or reconnect with the divine, *bhakti* means at the very least to recognize one's essential dependence on and participation in the divine. Participation takes the form of deep love: love of the deity for the living beings and love of the living beings for the deity. In this sense, one might think of *bhakti* as true knowledge which has deep ramifications for one's self-understanding and emotional experience. (Trans.)

[6]This is the first of the eight verses of instruction, called the *Śikṣāṣṭaka*, which are attributed to Śrī Caitanya (Trans.):

> चेतोदर्पणमर्जनं भवमहादावाग्निनिर्वापनम्
> श्रेयःकैरवचन्द्रिकावितरणं विद्यावधूजीवनम्।
> आनन्दाम्बुधिवर्धनं प्रतिपदं पूर्णामृतास्वादनम्
> सर्वात्मस्नपनं परं विजयते श्रीकृष्णसङ्कीर्तनम्॥

[7]These are the nine forms of *bhakti* mentioned in the *Bhāgavata Purāṇa* (7.5.23): hearing about, speaking about, remembering, serving the feet of, worshiping, praising, serving, becoming the friend of and offering oneself to Viṣṇu. (Trans.)

to bestow Kṛṣṇa himself.
Among those (nine), the best of all
is *saṅkīrtana* of the Name.
If one says the Name without offense,
one receives the treasure of love intensely."[8]

Although *saṅkīrtana* of the Holy Names is the practice of the age (*yuga-dharma*) in every Age of Kali, in this present age *saṅkīrtana* has a special trait and that is that this time he (Kṛṣṇa) has given it to the world with his own hand, infused with a shower of his own limitless compassion. Therefore it occupies a place of even greater magnificence, a magnificence for which there is no equal. As Śrī Jīva says in the *Bhakti-sandarbha*: "and in Kali, it is compassionately given by the Lord himself. Thus, its praise is comparatively greater."[9]

Śrī Gaura, taking a verse from the Sātvata scripture, the *Padma Purāṇa*, has given to the world the practice of the age, *saṅkīrtana* of the Holy Names, along with his own grace-filled commentary:

> The name of Hari, the name of Hari, only the name of Hari! In the Age of Kali, there is not, there is not, there is not another way.[10]

Kṛṣṇa descends in the Age of Kali
in the form of his Holy Name.[11]

---

[8]Kṛṣṇadāsadāsa Kavirāja, *Caitanya-caritāmṛta* (Cc), Antya, 4.70-71:

bhajaner madhye śreṣṭha navavidhā bhakti
kṛṣṇaprema kṛṣṇa dite dhare mahāśakti
tār madhye sarvaśreṣṭha nāmasaṅkīrtana
niraparādhe nāma laile pāya premadhana

[9]Śrī Jīva, Bs, 273: कलौ च श्रीभगवता कृपया तद्ग्राह्यत इत्यपेक्षयैव तत्र तत्प्रशंसेति स्थितम्

[10]Though the author gives this verse as from *Padma Purāṇa*, it is given in the *Hari-bhakti-vilāsa* as from the *Bṛhan-nāradīya Purāṇa*. No numbering is given there, but from another source the chapter and verse numbers are given as 38.126. (Trans.)

हरेर्नाम हरेर्नाम हरेर्नामैव केवलम् ।
कलौ नास्त्येव नास्त्येव नास्त्येव गतिरन्यथा ॥

[11]This is a word by word commentary on this important verse placed in the mouth of Śrī Caitanya himself by Kṛṣṇadāsa Kavirāja, author of the *Caitanya-caritāmṛta*. The verse in transliteration is: *harernāma harernāma harernāmaiva kevalam; kalau nāstyeva nāstyeva nāstyeva gatiranyathā.* (Trans.)

From his Holy Name comes
the salvation of all the world.
For emphasis *harernāma*[12]
is thrice repeated in this verse.
To make even dullards understand
there is again an *eva*.[13]
The word *kevala*[14] again
makes it even more certain.
Rejected are knowledge and *yoga*,
austerities and rites and the rest.
Whoever thinks otherwise is not delivered.
"Not!" "Not!" "Not!" and each with an *eva*.[15]

The followers of Śrī Gaura join their voices with that of their dear Lord's in praise of the Holy Name.

Sanātana Gosvāmin says:

> Kṛṣṇa! Slipping out of the threads of hearing (*śravaṇa*), you are again caught by the ropes of meditation (*dhyāna*). Escaping from those, too, you are captured by the chains of *saṅkīrtana* of your Name. Unsettled by *bhakti* for you, I will never let you go now that I have you. You are surrounded and tightly held, Wearer of Yellow Silk.[16]

---

[12] "the name of Hari (Viṣṇu-Kṛṣṇa)"

[13] That is, after the third *harernāma eva* is used. *Eva* is used to emphasize what immediately precedes it and generally means "indeed, for sure, alone." (Trans.)

[14] The last word of the first half of the verse. *Kevala* means "alone, only." (Trans.)

[15] Cc., Ādi, 17.19-22:

nāmarūpe kalikāle kṛṣṇa avatāra
nāma haite haya sarva jagat nistāra
dārḍhya lāgi harernāma ukti tin bāra
jaḍaloka bujhāite punar evakāra
kevalaśabda punarapi niścaya karaṇa
jñāna-yoga-tapa-karma-ādi nibāraṇa
anyathā ye māne tār nāhika nistāra
nāhi nāhi nāhi e tin evakāra

[16] Sanātana, *Bṛhad-bhāgavatāmṛta* (Bb), 2.1.1:

कृष्ण श्रवणपासात्त्वं निर्यातो ध्यानरज्जुभिः
ग्राह्यस्ताभ्यश्च निर्यातो नामकीर्तनशृङ्खलैः ।
त्वद्भक्तिलोलितेनाद्य न मया जातु मोक्ष्यसे

Here, following the teaching of a verse in the *Bhāgavata*,[17] the best of the various forms of *bhakti* is shown through a comparison of the strengths and weaknesses of *śravaṇa* (hearing), *kīrtana* (loud repetition),[18] and *smaraṇa* (remembering, visualization). If the *bhakti* of hearing is like binding with silk threads, the *bhakti* of remembering is like binding with cow ropes. And compared to that the *bhakti* of *kīrtana* is much more firm like binding with iron chains. Remembering pulls a mind absorbed in hearing away and makes it absorbed in remembering, and again *kīrtana* pulls a mind absorbed in remembering away and makes it fully absorbed in *kīrtana*. But *kīrtana* of the Holy Name effects such a firm binding that nothing else has the power to pull the mind away. In terms of power, the *kīrtana* of the Holy Name is the best of all; it has no equal. This has been shown here.

Śrī Jīva says, commenting on another verse in the *Bhāgavata*:[19]

> There, too, it is taught as the highest practice and the highest goal of all: this *saṅkīrtana* of the name of Hari is advocated

---

वृतो धृतोऽसि गाढं त्वं पीतकौशेयवाससि॥

[17]Bhāg. 2.1.5:

तस्माद्भारत सर्वात्मा भगवानीश्वरो हरिः।
श्रोतव्यः कीर्तितव्यश्च स्मर्तव्यश्चेच्छताऽभयम्॥

Therefore, Bhārata, Hari, who is the self of all, the lord and the controller, is to be heard about, proclaimed and remembered by anyone who desires fearlessness. (Trans.)

[18]Here the word *kīrtana* is used instead of *saṅkīrtana*. The difference between the two seems to be merely a matter of degree in presentation. In one place Jīva distinguishes between them by saying that *saṅkīrtana* is *kīrtana* with more than one person involved and that it is better than the latter because it brings about a special delight (*Bhakti-sandarbha*, 269, अत्र च बहुभिर्मिलित्वा कीर्तनं सङ्कीर्तनमित्युच्यते। तत्तु चमत्कारविशेषपोषात्पूर्वतोऽप्यधिकमिति ज्ञेयम्।). Sanātana says *saṅkīrtana* means "loud pronouncing" (*uccair uccārya*) and points out that it is done for one's own pleasure and that of others (comm. on Hbv 11.456, सङ्कीर्त्य सम्यगुच्चैरुच्चार्येति सद्यः स्वपरानन्दविशेषार्थमुक्तम्). In another place Sanātana says that *saṅkīrtana* is "vocalizing the Holy Name, songs and praises that consist of the Holy Names (comm. on Hbv, 11.458, सङ्कीर्तनं नामोच्चारणं गीतं स्तुतिश्च नाममयी). (Trans.)

[19]Bhāg., 2.1.11:

एतन्निर्विद्यमानानामिच्छतामकुतोभयम्।
योगिनां नृप निर्णीतं हरेर्नामानुकीर्तनम्॥

For yogis who are disgusted with this (world), who desire fearlessness, the repetition of the name of Hari is advocated, king. (Trans.)

> for those disgusted [with the material world].[20]

Saṅkīrtana of the Holy Names is the highest practice and the highest goal of all, of those desiring piety, wealth, sense enjoyment or liberation, as well as of the single-minded devotee.

Śrī Viśvanātha Cakravartin says in his commentary on that verse:[21]

> Although from scriptures like the *Bhāgavata* and others it is understood that *bhakti* is what is to be described (*abhidheya*) in them, the question arises which, among all the forms of *bhakti*, remembering etc., has been ascertained as the primary one. In answer it is said that *kīrtana* of the names of Hari that are dear to one has been recognized as the best of all, like an emperor above great kings. Among all the forms of *bhakti*, *śravaṇa*, *smaraṇa*, and *kīrtana* are the primary ones (vide Bhāg. 2.1.5). In this verse it is said that among those three, *kīrtana* is the main one. Again among the various forms of *kīrtana* (focusing on the names, the forms, the qualities, and the acts), *kīrtana* of the names is the best. Moreover, in this *kīrtana* of the names, *kīrtana* of names that fit one's own type of *bhakti* is considered the best of all. In other words, in the sweet (erotic) *rasa*,[22] for instance, pronouncing names like Gaura, Kṛṣṇa, Govinda, Rādhāramaṇa, Rādhā, and so forth, is the best. There is nothing equal or superior to it.[23]

In the present Age of Kali, all success comes without fail to those who travel the path of spiritual cultivation that was initiated and bestowed by Śrī Gaura, resting whole-heartedly and with deep respect in the knowledge that *kīrtana* of the Holy Name is the absolute best. On

[20] तत्रापि सर्वेषामेव परमसाधनत्वेन परमसाध्यत्वेन चोपदिशति — एतन्निर्विद्यमानानां हरेर्नाम-कीर्तनम्

[21] Bhāg., 2.1.11

[22] *Rasa* is the experience or "tasting" of one's fully developed love for Kṛṣṇa. It has five main varieties and seven minor varieties. The "sweet" (*madhura*) *rasa*, which is the erotic *rasa*, is considered the foremost of them all. See the Glossary for a more detailed discussion of *rasa* and its varieties. (Trans.)

[23] नन्वत्र शास्त्रे भक्तिरभिधेयेत्यवगम्यत एव। तत्रापि भक्त्यङ्गेषु मध्ये महाराजचक्रवर्तिवत्किमेकं मुख्यत्वेन निर्णीयते। तत्राह नामानुकीर्तनमिति। सर्वेषु भक्त्यङ्गेषु मध्ये श्रवणकीर्तनस्मरणानि त्रीणि मुख्यानि तस्माद्भारत इति श्लोकेनोक्तानि। तेषु त्रिष्वपि मध्ये कीर्तनम्, कीर्तनेऽपि नामलीलागुणादिसम्बन्धिनि तस्मिन्नामकीर्तनम्, तत्राप्यनुकीर्तनं स्वभक्त्यनुरूपनामकीर्तनम् (निरन्तरकीर्तनं वा) निर्णीतं पूर्वाचार्यैरपि न केवलं मयैवधुना निर्णीयत इति ।

the other hand, however, there really *is* no other way in this age for living beings to gain salvation. Śrī Gaurahari proclaimed this with his own lips, repeating the truth three times: *nāstyeva nāstyeva nāstyeva gatiranyathā*, "there is not, there is not, there is not another way." Therefore, Śrī Rūpa said, wishing the best for all the Vaiṣṇavas who follow him:

> May victory crown those syllables 'ha-re kṛ-ṣ-ṇa' bursting from the lips of Śrī Caitanya, which are his own names, flooding the whole world with love.[24]

Again, Śrī Rūpa, giving his blessings to the whole world, reveals his heart's special feeling:

> Name of Hari! The luster of the jewels on the crowns of all the Vedas illumine the tips of your lotus-like feet. I seek shelter completely, in every way, with you who are worshiped even by those who are already liberated.[25]

An item of particular note here is that Śrī Rūpa who is usually extremely measured with his words has used two words that have the same meaning in characterizing his taking wholeheartedly to the Holy Name: *paritas* and *saṃśrayāmi* which mean 'in every way' and 'I seek shelter *completely*,' respectively. The point of stating one idea twice is to make it clear that this subject is so important for the practitioner that if he does not grasp it, his entire life of practice will become useless. Therefore, the extremely compassionate Rūpa has stated it twice for emphasis.

Laghu: I understand that *saṅkīrtana* of the Holy Name is the best of all forms of worship, but some have an opposing opinion here, don't they? Is this conclusion only applicable to *vaidhī bhakti* (rule-motivated

---

[24] Rūpa Gosvāmin, *Laghu-bhāgavatāmṛta* (Lb), 4:

श्रीचैतन्यमुखोद्गीर्णा हरे कृष्णेतिवर्णिकाः ।
मज्जयन्तो जगत्प्रेम्नि विजयन्तां तदाह्वयाः ॥

[25] Rūpa, *Kṛṣṇa-nāmāṣṭaka*, 1:

निखिलश्रुतिमौलिरत्नमालाद्युतिनीराजितपादपङ्कजान्त ।
अयि मुक्तकुलैरुपास्यमानां परितस्त्वां हरिनाम संश्रयामि ॥

bhakti) or does it apply to *rāgānugā bhakti* (passion-pursuing *bhakti*), too?[26] Some say that in *rāgānugā bhakti, smaraṇa* (remembering, visualization) is the best.

Goswami: What some people say is not supported by the scriptures. Though in *rāgānugā bhakti smaraṇa* is indeed important, still, hierarchically speaking, important is not the final word. Beyond important there is more important, most important, and finally the 'fourth' (*turīya*). Viśvanātha Cakravartin makes such distinctions in his commentary on Karṇapūra's work, the *Ānanda-vṛndāvana-campū* ("Blissful Vṛndāvana").[27] In the world of spiritual cultivation (*sādhana*) the 'fourth' is *saṅkīrtana* of the Holy Names, than which there is nothing better.

In this connection, here are some of the considered conclusions of the Gosvāmins:

1.1 Viśvanātha Cakravartin's Conclusion

Viśvanātha has said that since *saṅkīrtana* of the Holy Name is the 'fourth' it is better than *smaraṇa* and all the rest and has called it the emperor among great kings in many places.[28] While agreeing that in *rāgānugā-bhakti smaraṇa* is of central importance, he has nevertheless compared *smaraṇa* with the commander-in-chief of the armed forces, beneath the emperor, *saṅkīrtana* of the Holy Name.

In the *Rāga-vartma-candrikā* (Moonlight on the Path of Passion) Viśvanātha says:

---

[26] *Vaidhī bhakti* is *bhakti* motivated by the rules or injunctions (*vidhi*) of scripture or, in other words, performed out of a sense of duty to the regulations of scripture. As Jīva puts it: "There are two kinds of *bhakti, vaidhī* and *rāgānugā*. The first is initiated by the rules given in scripture." (Bs. 235: भक्तिर्द्विविधा वैधी रागानुगा चेति। तत्र वैधी शास्त्रोक्तविधिना प्रवर्तिता।) *Rāgānugā bhakti* is *bhakti* motivated by the desire to have the kind of passionate love for Kṛṣṇa that is found in his close companions in Vraja. See the Glossary for a more detailed discussion. [Trans.]

[27] Avc, 14.53. This is just an example drawn from Kavi Karṇapūra's work to demonstrate the use of the word *turīya* to describe a state of excellence beyond the "best" or "main." सङ्गीतनिगमगमकचातुरीतुरीयाचार्या "teacher of the fourth order of expertise in deep natural tones in the art of music" and Viśvanātha's *ṭīkā*: तुरीया चतुर्थी मुख्या-मुख्यतरा-मुख्यतमा-तोऽप्यतिश्रेष्ठा इत्यर्थः, "*Turīyā* means 'fourth,' even better than important, more important, and most important." (Trans.)

[28] In his comm. on Bhāg. 2.1.11 and on Brs. 1.2.230.

> The subservience of *smaraṇa*, the central practice in *rāgānugā*, to *kīrtana* must also be emphasized because *kīrtana* has authority in this age and because it is established by all scriptures as the most excellent among all of the various paths of *bhakti*.[29]

Therefore, not just for rule-motivated (*vaidhī*), but for passion-pursuing (*rāgānugā*) *bhakti* too, *saṅkīrtana* of the Holy Names is the best.

1.2 Sanātana Gosvāmin's Conclusion

The preeminence of *saṅkīrtana* of the Holy Name in attaining the service of Rādhā, the highest prize of *rāgānugā-bhakti*, is shown in a comparative way quite clearly in one of the Gosvāmin's verses:

> That [service of Rādhā], made radiant by *saṅkīrtana* of the names of one's dearest, is attained by *bhakti* in which meditation on and singing about the various sports of Vraja are dominant. [30]

In his commentary on that verse Śrī Sanātana says:

> Now, the means of attaining the service of Rādhā is stated: "That ..." By ninefold *bhakti* in which remembering and singing of the various Gokula-sports of Śrī Kṛṣṇa predominate, *preman* (sacred love)[31] is easily achieved. The one qualification that there is in this matter is stated next: *preman* is manifested or clarified by *saṅkīrtana* of the names of one's desired lord or the names of the lord that are most dear to one. Although in using the word *gāna* [song], *saṅkīrtana* of the Holy

---

[29] अत्र रागानुगाय यन्मुख्यस्य तस्यापि कीर्तनाधीनत्वमवश्यं वक्तव्यमेव कीर्तनस्यैव एतद्युगाधिकारत्वात्सर्वभक्तिमार्गेषु सर्वशास्त्रैस्तस्यैव सर्वोत्कर्षप्रतिपादनाच्च

[30] Bb, 2.5.218:

> तद्धि तत्तद्व्रजक्रीडाध्यानगानप्रधानया ।
> भक्त्या सम्पद्यते प्रेष्ठनामसङ्कीर्तनोज्ज्वलम् ॥

[31] *Preman* is the divine love that is the desired objective of the Caitanya tradition. It is self-less love aimed at pleasing fully the person who is the object of that love. See the Glossary for a more detailed account of the nature of *preman*. (Trans.)

> Name is included, *saṅkīrtana* of the names most dear to one has been mentioned again in particular. The reason for that is that compared to meditating on and singing of the Vraja sports, *saṅkīrtana* of the Holy Names is a comparatively more intimate means to *preman*, more primary than the primary, that than which there is nothing better.[32]

Or, *saṅkīrtana* of the beloved's Holy Name is itself the very essence of the attainment of *preman*.

1.3 The Easiest Way?

Why is the Holy Name the easiest way to attain immortality? That one discovers among the first principles of the Holy Name.[33] Now listen to those principles of the Holy Name.

---

[32]तत्रैव विशेषमाह प्रेष्ठस्य निजेष्टतमदेवस्य प्रेष्ठानां वा निजप्रियतमानां भगवन्नाम्नां सङ्कीर्तनेन उज्ज्वलं प्रकाशमानं शुद्धं वा ।गानेत्युक्त्वा नामकीर्तने प्राप्तेऽपि निजप्रियतमनामकीर्तनस्य प्रेमान्तरङ्गतरसाधनत्वेन पुनर्विशेषेण निर्देशः किंवा तत्सम्पत्तिलक्षणज्ञानाय

[33]This is *nāma-tattva* in the original. I have translated it as 'first principles of the Holy Name." It might also be translated "truths of the Holy Name." *Tattva* means "thatness, the way things are in essense." [Trans.]

Chapter 2

First Principles of the Holy Name

Goswami: Just as iron when in contact with fire gains the qualities of fire, we, too, by contact with an immortal substance are able to become immortal. That immortal substance is the Holy Name.

> A wish-granting gem is the Holy Name;
> it is Kṛṣṇa himself indeed,
> informed juice (*rasa*) of consciousness,
> full,[1] pure,[2] and eternally freed,[3]
> since Name and Named are forever the same.[4]

Śrī Jīva in a commentary on this verse has said:

> The Holy Name is a wish-granting gem (*cintāmaṇi*): it grants all one's desires.[5] Since the Holy Name is Kṛṣṇa himself, it

[1]Undivided.

[2]Free of connection with māyā.

[3]Beyond the power of māyā.

[4]*Padma Purāṇa*:

> नाम चिन्तामणिः कृष्णश्चैतन्यरसविग्रहः ।
> पूर्णः शुद्धो नित्यमुक्तोऽभिन्नत्वान्नामनामिनोः ॥

[5]That is, while one is in contact with the Holy Name, whose very nature is truth, whatever one thinks comes true. Therefore, it is called a wishing gem. See Bhāg., 11.15.26: *yathā saṅkalpayet*.

> has the nature of Kṛṣṇa. Consciousness and so forth are qualifiers of Kṛṣṇa. The reason the Holy Name is Kṛṣṇa is that the Name and the Named are not different. *One eternal, conscious, blissful, delectable truth has appeared as two.*[6]

Joyful astonishment is called *rasa*. This *rasa* is consciousness-*rasa* — it has no relationship with *māyā*. It is as though a syrup (*rasa*), poured into two molds, one a human-like form and the other a syllabic form, solidified into two forms. One is the human form — Śyāmasundara (Beautiful Dark One), Vaṃśīdhārī (Bearer of a Flute), Tribhaṅgī (Bent Three Ways) — and the other is the ultimate syllabic form, 'kṛṣṇa.' The two are embodied consciousness-*rasa*, the highest ambrosia,[7] a condensed ocean of the highest joy.[8] The Holy Name possesses a full form.[9]

In the words of Śrī Sanātana Gosvāmin, whose very life and ornament was the Holy Name, the highest ambrosia, the principle of the Holy Name was expressed in a rapturous outburst:

> Indeed! The Name of Kṛṣṇa is an extremely elevated, *rasa*-filled thing. Why *rasa*-filled? Because it is soft, being composed of sweet syllables, or, because it is made of the *rasa* of eternal being, consciousness, and joy (*saccidānanda*); it is *rasa*-filled. Or, because it is present with unlimited kinds of *rasa*, appearing in the nine *rasas* headed by *śṛṅgāra*, in the *rasa* of *bhakti*, in the *rasa* of *preman* (love) and in the conditions of separation [from Kṛṣṇa] and union [with Kṛṣṇa]; therefore it is *rasa*-filled. Or, *rasa* means passion for the deity (*rāga*); this Name, joined with such passion, without fail brings about love of the Lord. Therefore this Name is *rasa*-filled. Or, the Name creates in the minds of its servants or of everyone an attraction for itself; therefore it is *rasa*-filled. Or, *rasa* can be understood as a kind of efficacy that this Name possesses. It has the greatest of powers; therefore it is *rasa*-filled. Or,

---

[6] Jīva's comm. on Brs., 1.2.233: नामैव चिन्तामणिः सर्वाभीष्टदायकं यतस्तदेव कृष्णः कृष्णस्य स्वरूपमित्यर्थः। कृष्णस्य विशेषणानि चैतन्यादीनि तस्य कृष्णत्वे हेतुरभिन्नत्वादिति। एकमेव सच्चिदानन्दरसादिरूपं तत्त्वं द्विविधाविर्भूतमित्यर्थः।

[7] Sanātana Gosvāmin says at Bb, 1.1.9 : परमामृतमेकं जीवनं भूषणं मे, "It [the Name] is highest ambrosia, my only life and ornament."

[8] Rūpa, *Kṛṣṇa-nāmāṣṭaka*: रम्यचिद्घनसुखस्वरूपिणे, "[to the Name] whose essential nature is the joy of beautiful, condensed consciousness."

[9] Rūpa, *Kṛṣṇa-nāmāṣṭaka*: पूर्णवपुषे नमो नमः, "obeisances again and again to the Name whose body is full."

> *rasa* can refer to a special quality — this Name delivers all distressed people; therefore it is *rasa*-filled.[10]

It is as if Śrī Sanātana imbibed so much *rasa* that his outburst will never end. Therefore he continues on:

> If *rasa* is a kind of happiness, since the Name is made of condensed happiness, therefore it is *rasa*-imbued. Or, if *rasa* is sweetness, since the Name is sweetness at its highest limit, supremely sweet, it is *rasa-imbued*. As it is said "sweeter than sweet, extremely sweet;" therefore nothing else is equal to it. It is incomparable.[11]

The Named himself and the syllables of the Name are without dependence on anything else, fully, that is, completely, non-different in power and in sweetness. They are like a mango and an apple that are both molded from solid sugar; independently they are the same in taste, aroma and sweetness.

Therefore, even though Ajāmila was completely devoid of any connection with the Named, Nārāyaṇa, the Lord of Vaikuṇṭha, at the time he called his own son, also named Nārāyaṇa, he got sudden liberation as a result of the contact of his tongue with those four syllables.[12]

Furthermore, in Rūpa's play, the *Vidagdha-mādhava* (Clever Mādhava), his character Paurṇamāsī says: *no jāne janitā kiyadbhiramṛtaiḥ kṛṣṇetivarṇa-dvayī*: "I don't know how much ambrosia the two syllables '*kṛṣ-ṇa*' are made of." This is the sweetness of the Holy Name. "One truth, consisting of eternal being, consciousness, joy, *rasa* and so forth, has appeared

---

[10]Sanātana, comm. on Bb., 2.3.184: यतः सरसं कोमलं मधुराक्षरमयत्वात् सच्चिदानन्दरसमयत्वाद्वा। यद्वा रसैरशेषैरेव सह वर्तमानं शृङ्गारादिनवरसेषु भक्तिरसे प्रेमरसे च तथा विरहसङ्गमयोश्च परिस्फुरणात्। यद्वा रसो रागस्तत्सहितमव्यभिचारितेनावश्यमेवाशु श्रीभगवत्प्रेमसम्पादनात्। यद्वा स्वस्मिन् स्वसेवकानां सर्वेषां वा जनानामनुरागजनकत्वात्। यद्वा रसो वीर्यविशेषः परमशक्तिमत्वात्। यद्वा गुणविशेषोऽखिलदीनजननिस्तारकत्वात्।

[11]ibid.: यद्वा सुखविशेषः घनसुखमयत्वात्। माधुर्यविशेषो वा परममधुरत्वादिति दिक्। यथोक्तं मधुरमधुरेत्यादि। अतस्तस्य नाम्न एव समं तत्तुल्यमन्यत् किञ्चिन्नास्तीति निरुपममित्यर्थः॥

[12]This refers to the Story of Ajāmila told in the Sixth Canto, Second Chapter of the *Bhāgavata Purāṇa*. Ajāmila though he was not a devotee of Viṣṇu called on his death bed for his son who was named Nārāyaṇa. Since he uttered the name of Viṣṇu as he died, even though he was referring to his son, he was liberated from rebirth by Viṣṇu. This is one of the primary examples of the power of the semblance or *ābhāsa* of the Name. See the Glossary for more details on *ābhāsa*. [Trans.]

as two."[13] This statement of Śrī Jīva, in his discussion of the Holy Name, is the definitive word. It has authority everywhere, or, in other words, it is the conclusion.

The Holy Name is a Vaikuṇṭha substance (Bhāg. 6.2.14) — that is, a substance always without weakness (*kuṇṭha*) — it does not become impure in any condition — it does not not become corrupted by incursion of the faults of an offender, nor in the semblance (*ābhāsa*) of the Name is it changed.[14]

2.1 The Holy Name: its Compassion and Generosity

Laghu: If the Holy Name is a condensed ocean of the highest joy then just as when one places one's hand on a large block of ice and immediately goose-bumps arise at the infusion of its quality of coldness throughout the body, by mere contact with the Holy Name goose-bumps should arise in our bodies at the infusion of the great joy of the Holy Name. But that doesn't happen. Why not?

Goswami: Just think a little. Does the hand always feel the cold when it is placed on a block of ice? It doesn't. It depends on the condition of the hand. If the hand is covered with a thick covering of cork, it will not feel any of the cold at all. The degree of experience of cold depends on the degree of the hand's covering. In the same way, the degree of our experience of that great joy depends on the degree of our offense. If one's offense is as hard as a quilt of diamonds then one will not experience any joy at all and visa-versa.

Laghu: Very well, I can accept that. Offense deprives us of tasting the joy. Still, the point is that the need for the gifts of the generous is greater for penniless, fallen low-lifes like us. If those gifts don't reach us then what is so great about that charity? In other words, what is the use of calling such a giver a 'wish-granting gem,' 'bestower of all one's desires,' and so on?

---

[13] From Jīva's comm. on Brs. 1.2.233.

[14] Vaikuṇṭa really means sharp, not dull or blunt or stupid. It is the word often applied to Viṣṇu's heaven, the spiritual realm in Vaiṣṇava theology. Here it means simply spiritual or other-worldly, not from the material realm, not corruptible by the influences of that realm. See the glossary for more details. [Trans.]

Goswami: There is One, the crown-jewel of givers, a veritable ocean of mercy, whose compassion has no limit and of whose compassion even offenders, the bad, the lowest, the outcasts are not deprived; that is the Holy Name. Even when that ocean of great compassion, the Named himself, is put off by the foul smell of the rubbish in the courtyard-like heart of a sinful offender and stands at a distance, this Holy Name willingly accepts the lowly work of a sweeper, and sweeping out that courtyard, gradually makes it clean and pure. Then the Holy Name comes and sits down to rest in that pure, peaceful, temple of the heart, washed in the holy waters of the Gaṅgā. (Narottama Dāsa sings: "in the hearts of the holy, ever Govinda rests") Then one can see: the Holy Name is greater in compassion and generosity than even the Named himself. Even though the Holy Name and the Holy Named are entirely non-different, the Holy Name is distinguished by having greater compassion and generosity. The Holy Name understands the condition of everyone and distributes compassion equally. The offenses of the offender dwindle and the self-less love (*preman*) of those who are offenseless increases. A typhoon arises in such a person's ocean of love (*preman*) during daily respectful *saṅkīrtana* of the Holy Name.[15]

Laghu: Yet some contemporary people say that supernatural (*aprākṛta*) *bhakti* can never come into the refuse of the natural senses. Along with becoming prepared for or engaged in service, the senses become supernatural and to those supernatural senses supernatural *bhakti* can come. They cite the *Bhakti-rasāmṛta-sindhu* as evidence for this position. Rūpa says there:

> Therefore, the names and so forth of Kṛṣṇa cannot be grasped by the senses. When one is ready for service, they appear themselves on the tongue and the rest.[16]

But you said previously that the Holy Name comes to the natural senses and gradually after a while in contact with *bhakti* the senses be-

[15] Viśvanātha Cakravartin, comm. on Bhāg., 6.3.24: तस्मात्सङ्कीर्तनं विष्णोरिति अनुदिनमिदमादरे शृण्वनित्यादिषु भक्तेरनेकेषामङ्गानां श्रद्धावृत्तिसम्यत्क्कादेरपि यद्विधानं तन्निरपराधानां प्रेमवृद्ध्यर्थम्। नामापराधवतां तु नामापराधक्षयार्थञ्च।

[16] Brs., 1.2.234:

> अतः श्रीकृष्णनामादि न भवेद्ग्राह्यमिन्द्रियैः।
> सेवोन्मुखे हि जिह्वादौ स्वयमेव स्फुरत्यदः॥

come supernatural. What is the real meaning of scripture on this issue?[17]

Goswami: Listen carefully to what Viśvanātha Cakravartin has said on this issue. All of your doubts will be dispelled, and there will be no need for me to say anything more.

> [*Pūrvapakṇa*:][18] All right, *preman* (divine love) is without any material quality, but how can a mental event be without material quality? One may claim that a relationship of container and contained (*ādhāra-ādheya*) exists between the mind and the divine love in the mind. But then even the mental events of a practitioner who has not yet developed love (*ajāta-rati*), whose worship in fact has barely begun, would have to be considered free of material quality because it "contains" *bhakti* (which is without material quality). How then can things like anger, hatred, and so forth be present in his mind as obstacles to *bhakti*?
>
> Well put. One cannot say here that the mind becomes free of material qualities through the relationship of container-contained. Rather, it happens without that. The conclusion of scripture is like this: by its merely entering the ears and other senses in the form of *kīrtana* of the Holy Name and so forth, no mixing of the senses with *bhakti* occurs. Rather, in the uninterrupted burnishing or grinding of *bhakti* against the material mind through repetitive practice, after advancing through the stages of cessation of harmful habits (*anartha-nivṛtti*), stability (*niṣṭhā*), liking (*ruci*) and attachment (*āsakti*),[19]

[17]The way that some interpret the verse is not warranted by scripture. Śrī Jīva in his commentary on this verse says that the meaning of "being ready for service" is: *bhagavatsvarūpatannāmagrahaṇāya pravṛttaḥ*, "engaged in repeating his name which is of the essential nature of the Lord." In accordance with this, the meaning of the verse is: "since Kṛṣṇa's names are of his essential nature, they cannot be grasped by the power of the senses. If, however, the tongue and other senses become engaged in repeating the names and the rest, the names themselves come and appear in those senses."

[18]*Pūrva-pakṣa* means the previous or opposing viewpoint, real or imagined. It is the position that the author will argue against in his rejoinder. Often times the viewpoint is that of a strawman invented to bring home the point the author wants to emphasize. Sometimes however the previous position represents an actual opposing view held by a real opposing party. It is a testimony to the sophistication of the art of debate in India that one must know well the position of one's opponents and be able to state it clearly as part of the *pūrvapakṣa*.

[19]These are some of the earlier stages in the gradual development of *bhakti* that Rūpa recognizes in his *Bhakti-rasāmṛtasindhu*(1.4.15-16). The three prior stages are faith (*śraddhā*),

> a union between them [the senses and *bhakti*] takes place. As long as there is no mixing, the mundane conditions of lust, anger, and so forth remain in the mind able to cause harm.[20]

By merely adding mercury to sulphur powder no real union takes place between them. But, with repeated mixing, union does occur after a while. Furthermore, just as when union occurs, sulphur's own form disappears and it takes on another form, so is the mundane condition of the mind destroyed and it becomes spiritualized (*cinmaya*, transformed into *cit* or consciousness). Just as in the union of sulphur and mercury a new thing, mascara (*kohl*), is produced, so in the mixing of *bhakti* with the mind *preman* is produced.

In his commentary on the 10th Canto of the *Bhāgavata Purāṇa*, Viśvanātha Cakravartin has even more clearly made this point:

> The body of the devotee at first is a mixture of material quality (*guṇa*) and absense of material quality (*nirguṇa*). To the degree that *bhakti* gradually increases, the material quality part decreases and quality-less part increases. On the stage of *preman* material quality is completely destroyed and the quality-less condition becomes complete.[21]

It is just like a mango that is at first slightly reddened, then half ripened, and finally fully ripened.

Sanātana Gosvāmin has said the very same thing in the statement "even of those having bodies made of the five elements ... :"

> With the appearance of *bhakti*, [in the course of time] the body composed of five elements obtains the form of eternal being, consciousness, and joy (*saccidānanda*). Moreover, by

---

association with the holy (*sādhusaṅga*) and performance of worship (*bhajana-kriyā*). They lead through the stages mentioned here to strong emotional attraction (*bhāva, kṛṣṇa-rati*) and finally to love (*preman*). [Trans.]

[20] Viśvanātha Cakravartin, comm. on Un., 9.28: तथाहि प्रथमं स्वानामित्यादिरीत्या भक्तेः कर्णप्रवेशमात्रेणैव झटति न तेन मेलनं स्यात्। किन्तु निरन्तरमन्तःकरणेन सह भक्तेरभ्यासः पौनःपुन्येनानर्थनिवृत्तिनिष्ठारुच्यासक्तिभूमिकारोहनान्तरमेव। यावच्च तया न मेलनं स्यात्तावन्मनोवृत्तयो रागद्वेषादय प्राकृता अनर्थकरा एव।

[21] Viśvanātha Cakravartin, comm on Bhāg., 10.29.10: भक्तदेहस्यांशेन निर्गुणत्वगुणमयत्वञ्च स्यात्। भक्तिवृद्धितारतम्येन निर्गुणदेहांशानामाधिक्यतारतम्यं स्यात्। प्रेम्ण्युत्पन्ने तु गुणमयदेहांशेषु नष्टेषु सम्यङ्निर्गुण एव देहः स्यात्।

> the force of her power of compassion, Bhakti-devi is able to appear in any condition [that is, even in a body of the material elements].[22]

Laghu: Śrī Cakravartin in his commentary has spoken of repeated burnishing or grinding. But isn't anything quickly possible by the power of the thing itself without that grinding?

Goswami: Yes, it is possible for it to happen quickly by the power of the thing itself. Still, that is not a common occurence. It is uncommon, as for instance in the case of success by grace in which by Kṛṣṇa's grace or by that of his devotee, even without practice, love arises (see Brs., 1.2.15). Again in the *Bṛhad-bhāgavatāmṛta* Sanātana Gosvāmin has said: "the holy land's power is limitless. By its mercy even without practice some are able to attain the goal."[23] Do you know what this is like? It is like finding money by chance. If, after hearing that someone has found money, we tie up our waist cloths and sit in our rooms, making no effort to earn it, then it is almost certain that we will die of starvation. We have to bring about the descent of his grace through intense practice. Worship depends upon effort.

It can also happen quickly for someone who is without offense.

> The top five forms of *bhakti*, headed by the Holy Name, have a hard-to-comprehend power indeed; forget about having faith for the moment, even by merely deciding to undertake them those whose minds are free of offense obtain love.[24]

Jīva Gosvāmin in his commentary has defined the word *sad-dhiyām* as "those whose minds are free of offense." As soon as a person free from offense pronounces the Holy Name or touches the dust of the holy land, that person will be overcome with feelings that produce tears, trembling, gooseflesh and so forth. But the sad thing is that we living beings in the age of Kali are almost all gripped by offense, whether large or small. Therefore, none of this happens quickly for us. We need the repeated burnishing.

---

[22] Sanātana Gosvāmin, comm. on Bb., 2.3.139: पाञ्चभौतिकदेहवतामपि भक्तिस्फूर्त्या सच्चिदानन्दरूपतायामेव पर्यवसनात्, किंवा तत्कारुण्यशक्तिविशेषेण तत्र तत्रापि तत्स्फूर्तिसम्भवात्।

[23] Bb., 1.1.4?

[24] Brs., 1.2.238:

> दुरूहाद्भुतवीर्येऽस्मिन् श्रद्धा दूरेऽस्तु पञ्चके।
> यत्र सङ्कल्पोऽपि सम्बन्धः सद्धियां भावजन्मने॥

2.2 The Semblance (*Ābhāsa*) of the Holy Name

Laghu: What is the *ābhāsa* of the Holy Name?

Goswami: The meaning of the word *ābhāsa* is "vague or dim manifestation." Śrī Sanātana Gosvāmin has glossed *ābhāsa* with the word "imitating" (*anukāraka*, ie., having the same form as something else in the manner of a reflection). It is like the relationship between the sun, which is the original, and its image in water, which is its reflection.

In scripture the following discussion of *ābhāsa* of the Holy Name is found:

1. It is the first unfolding of the Holy Name in the mind of a practitioner engaged in cultivating the Holy Name, like the early stages of the rising of the sun. (When the Holy Name is not present on the tongue, but is in the mind, it is *ābhāsa* of the Holy Name. When it is present on the tongue, too, it is the Holy Name itself, not a semblance.)[25] (Cc, Antya 3.182-85)

[25]It is not clear what Manindranath Babu means here nor where he got this idea. If he means that when the Holy Name begins to manifest itself as a result of the practitioner's diminishing offenses, its first reflections appear in the mind of the practitioner and then later the Name itself appears on the tongue of the practitioner, I am unaware of the foundation for such a belief in Caitanya Vaiṣṇavism. Certainly, the passage he cites from the *Caitanya-caritāmṛta* immediately following says nothing of the idea. If he means that the Holy Name chanted in the mind is merely semblance, whereas the Holy Name chanted on the tongue, that is audibly, is the Name itself, he is probably wrong. Numerous modern practitioners would disagree with him. It appears that one major source for this understanding that *nāmābhāsa* is the "first rays" of the sunlike Holy Name which about to rise in the mind of the practitioner seems to be a verse from the *Padma Purāṇa* cited by Rūpa Gosvāmin in his *Bhakti-rasāmṛta-sindhu*, 2.1.103:

तं निर्व्याजं भज गुणनिधे पावनं पावनानां
श्रद्धारज्यन्मतिरतितरामुत्तमःश्लोकमौलिम् ।
प्रोद्यन्नन्तःकरणकुहरे हन्त यन्नामभानो-
राभासोऽपि क्षपति महापातकध्वान्तधाराम् ॥

Ocean of good qualities! With your mind illumined by faith you should worship him free from all insincerity, him who is the purifier of purifiers, the crown of those praised by the finest verse, the reflection (*ābhāsa*) of whose sunlike name rising in the cave of the mind destroys the flood of darkness

2. If the Holy Named is joined with a living being through the syllables of the Holy Name in an incidental way, completely without expectation, it is *ābhāsa* of the Holy Name. Examples:

    (a) The story of Ajāmila who in calling his son named Nārāyaṇa pronounced the word "nārāyaṇa." This is elsewhere called conventional (*saṅketa*) *ābhāsa*of the Holy Name.

    (b) The story of Satyatapas in the *Varāha Purāṇa* cited in Sanātana's commentary on *Bṛhad-bhāgavatāmṛta* (2.2.173). A *brāhmaṇa* was standing in water doing his daily prayers. At that time a tiger who was about to attack him was struck by the arrow of a hunter and was liberated on hearing in his dying moment the Holy Name from the mouth of the *brāhmaṇa*. This is an example of liberation by the *ābhāsa* of the Holy Name.

Nearly all of Kali's living beings are in the grips of some measure of offense. As a result *ābhāsa* of the Holy Name has no effect on them (*Krama-sandarbha*, 6.2.20). What then is the purpose of discussing *ābhāsa* of the Holy Name? It is discussed in order to give at least some sense of the indescribable, unlimited power of the Holy Name.

The statement in scripture that by one *ābhāsa* of the Holy Name one gets liberation and a little later attains Vaikuṇṭha applies in a case of absence of offense to the Holy Name. When there is offense, *ābhāsa* of the Holy Name has no effect. In the latter case, one must depend on practice or repetition. The Name itself clears away the sins and offenses of a person possessed of offense to the Holy Name. If one is tirelessly engaged in chanting, the Holy Name will be effective. As it is said in the *Padma Purāṇa*: *nāmāparādhayuktānāṃ nāmānyeva harantyagham*, " the Names themselves carry away the sins of those who are offenders of the Holy Names."[26] One should take the words *nāmāny eva* to mean "only the Holy Name," or "the *ābhāsa* of the Holy Name," but not any thing else.

---

that consists of great sin.

Here is it said that the reflection of the Holy Name, which is compared with the sun, rises in the mind and destroys the darkness of great sin there. Though this does connect the reflection of the Holy Name with the mind as does Manindra Babu, no commentator on the verse has suggested the rest of what Manibabu says here. [Trans.]

[26]Jīva, *Krama-sandarbha* on Bhāg. 6.2.20: अत्र साङ्केत्यमित्यादौ सकृन्नामाभासेनापि यन्निःशेषाघधुननोक्त्या वासनापर्यन्तक्षयमुच्यते। गुणानुवाद इत्यादौ तु भक्त्यावृत्त्यैवेति यत्तत्तु यथाक्रमं नामापराधशून्यतद्युक्तभजनापेक्षया ज्ञेयम्। नमापराधयुक्तानां नामान्येव हरन्त्यघम् । अविश्रान्तप्रयुक्तानि तान्येवार्थकराणीतिपाद्मात्।

Here is the victory flag of the blessing of Gaura — without his grace there was no other way for the living beings of the Age of Kali, because we had lost the ability even to take our medicine. We are profoundly offensive. It was a case of the Holy Name, our one and only medicine, not coming to our tongues. Before the coming of Gaura, the Holy Name did not come — Śrī Vālmīki is an example of that. At first the name of Rāma would not come to Ratnākara's tongue. But now the situation is different — now, if anyone desires to repeat the Holy Name, that Name, out of the greatest compassion, comes and dances on his tongue, the mirror of his mind is cleansed, and gradually that servant of the ambrosia of the Name becomes immersed in the ocean of the ambrosia of *preman*.

Chapter 3

Offenses to the Holy Name

Laghu: What is an offense to the Holy Name?

Goswami: The only cause of missing out on the grace of the merciful Holy Name is displeasing it, otherwise known as *aparādha* or offense. That which brings about the displeasure of the Holy Name, causing its pleasure (*rādha*) to vanish (*apa*), is called an offense to the Holy Name. The displeased Holy Name contracts its power to protect the sheltered.[1]

Laghu: Then along with learning of the greatness and sweetness of the Holy Name one needs to learn especially well about the hard-to-control power of offense to the Holy Name. Please graciously describe that to me.

Goswami: Just as the Holy Name's power is limitless — if one intentionally or unintentionally does *kīrtana* of the Holy Name, all of one's sins are uprooted — so is the power of offense to the Holy Name limitless. If one knowingly or unknowingly even brushes against an offense to the Holy Name, the love of even a great devotee is destroyed. The action of an offense is that gradually attraction [for Kṛṣṇa] is destroyed and one begins to regard the spiritual as material. The great ones have by their examples given us warnings in this thoroughly destructive matter.

---

[1] Viśvanātha on Bhāg. 6.2.9-10: यदि ते अपराधिनस्स्युरिति तस्याप्रसाद एव स्वाश्रितापालने कारणम् ।

One day, while the beloved devotee of Nṛsiṃhadeva,[2] Prahlāda,[3] was engaged in the service of Viṣṇu, a guard came and delivered the news, "two Vaiṣṇava have come to see you and are waiting at the door." King Prahlāda then requested him with folded hands: "Please ask the Vaiṣṇava to wait for a little bit." Then in the absorption of performing rites of worship for his image, he forgot about those Vaiṣṇava. The Vaiṣṇava waited for quite a while and then, blaming their bad fortune, left. Meanwhile, the great offense of disrespecting Vaiṣṇava touched the heart of Prahlāda and suddenly his mind reversed poles. He became disfigured with anger and began to say: "Viṣṇu is the enemy of my father. He is on the side of the gods who are opposed to us; they are long-standing enemies of our clan. Today I am going to attack Vaikuṇṭha and punish them." Throughout the clans of demons the words "Prepare! Prepare!" reverberated. Outfitting a huge army Prahlāda went to conquer Vaikuṇṭha. Just see what great trouble can rise from just one offense. Fortunately, by his guru's mercy, Prahlāda Mahārāja was protected from that course.[4]

Śrī Rūpa Gosvāmin has also given us an example in this matter. One day he went into a trance remembering the sacred play (*līlā*) of Rādhā and Kṛṣṇa. He was watching Śrī Kṛṣṇa lift Rādhā with both hands to collect flowers from a high branch of a tree. Suddenly Kṛṣṇa released her and Rādhā, grabbing the branch, was left dangling there. Seeing this trick the girlfriends all began to laugh and along with them Śrī Rūpa in his vision. At that very moment a crippled Vaiṣṇava happened to be passing in front of Rūpa. He thought "Gosvāmī is laughing at me" and became sad. Because of that Vaiṣṇava's sadness an offense touched Śrī Rūpa's heart and his vision was broken. The sacred play did not appear in his heart any more. See how one offense is able to spread subtly its web of harm. Anyway, later on that crippled Vaiṣṇava undertood the truth of Rūpa's laughter and his mental balance returned. Śrī Rūpa was able to return to his meditations.

Laghu: What incredible power offense has! How does the displeasing of or offense to the Holy Name occur? Kindly tell me about this.

Goswami: One can know how the Holy Name becomes displeased from verses beginning with the "Blasphemy of the holy ... " (*satāṃ nindā*

---

[2]The half lion, half man descent of Kṛṣṇa.

[3]Prahlāda was a great devotee of Nṛsiṃha from the community often referred to as "demons" (*asura*). That identification arises from their often being depicted in the Purāṇas as in conflict with the *devas* or gods. [Trans.]

[4]The source of this story is unknown. No more details are available at present. [Trans.]

nāmnaḥ) of the *Padma Purāṇa*.[5] Ten kinds of offense are listed there. Listen to Śrī Jīva's discussion in his commentary, the *Krama-sandarbha*, on *Bhāgavata* verse 2.1.11.

1. **Blasphemy of the Good or Virtuous.** It is a fault to blaspheme any living being. That is a general fault, however, not an offense to the Holy Name. Faith is the doorway through which one enters the world of *bhakti*. "A person who has faith is qualified for *bhakti*."[6] "By the word faith one means trust, a firm certainty that if one performs *bhakti* to Kṛṣṇa all actions are thereby accomplished."[7] With the appearance of this state of mind one's being a Vaiṣṇava begins. Such Vaiṣṇava through whom the glory of the Holy Name is spread in the world are the "good" or the "virtuous" (*sādhu*). Blasphemy of such virtuous persons, or nourishing a feeling of hostility towards them, or not welcoming them or not being pleased when one sees them is the most egregious of offenses to the Holy Name. Therefore, it is listed first. Even hearing blasphemy of the virtuous is an offense to the Holy Name.

2. **Thinking Śiva is Independent of Viṣṇu.** After becoming the Womb-water-lying (Gabhodayaśayī) Mahāviṣṇu[8] who is but a portion of the Causal-water-lying (Kāraṇodaśayī) Mahāviṣṇu

[5] *Padma Purāṇa*, Sarga, 48.46-49.

[6] Cc., Madhya, 22.64: *śraddhāvān jana haya bhakti adhikārī.*

[7] Cc., Madhya, 22.62: *śraddhā śabde viśvāsa kahe sudṛḍha niścaya, kṛṣṇe bhakti kaile sarvakarmakṛta haya.*

[8] According to the Vaiṣṇava theology derived from the Pāñcarātra school, Kṛṣṇa first expands into the form known as Saṅkarṣaṇa ("the one who draws or holds together"). Saṅkarṣaṇa creates or manifests both the spiritual and material worlds. In the process of creating the material world he expands into the form known as Kāraṇodaśayī ("Causal-water-lying") Viṣṇu who lies in a great ocean of causality (or material potentiality) and goes into a yogic trance (*yoga-nidrā*, lit. yoga-sleep). From the pores of his skin innumerable golden bubbles arise in that ocean and into each of them he enters in another form, the form known as Garbhodaśayī ("Womb-water-lying") Viṣṇu. He fills half of each bubble with his sweat and lies down in the resulting water. He then expands into the Quality Descents (Viṣṇu, Brahmā and Śiva), that is, the descents that reflect each of the material qualities: goodness (bright, clear), darkening (dimness), and darkness. He darkness-quality descent is Śiva whose work in the universe is to bring about its eventual destruction. Thus, in this tradition, Śiva is viewed as a mediated descent of Viṣṇu that has been transformed through contact with the quality of darkness or inertia. Nevertheless, he is fundamentally not different from Viṣṇu and certainly not to be thought of as independent of or separate from Viṣṇu. Rūpa has described this progression of expansions in his *Laghu-bhāgavatāmṛta* 2.7-33, quoting from the *Sātvata-tantra*, the *Brahma-saṃhitā*, and the *Bhāgavata Purāṇa*. [Trans.]

who, in turn, is but a portion of Kṛṣṇa's own form called Saṅkarṣaṇa, Śrī Kṛṣṇa, in order to destroy the world, takes on the material quality of darkness (the *tamo-guṇa*) and becomes the Quality Descent (*guṇa-avatāra*) known as Śiva. It is like the turning of milk into yogurt.[9] Those who think that this Śiva is an independent principle are offenders of the Holy Name. One should look at Śiva as the best devotee of the Lord and respect him.[10] Harihara (Viṣṇu-Śiva) are one being — that is, in their dearness.[11]

3. **Neglecting or Disrespecting the Guru**. The guru is the teacher who teaches one about the spiritual world, a protector and a friend — even more affectionate than one's father. The Lord descends distributively, that is, in many individual forms, as a devotee and is present in the world as the individual guru. At the same time, in the spiritual realm, the guru exists eternally in his collective or unitary form as a direct descent [of Kṛṣṇa] situated at the left side of the Lord.[12] For this reason, in the guru both the form of Kṛṣṇa and the form of the best devotee of Kṛṣṇa simultaneously coexist.[13] The Lord is manifest through some devotee who loves him as the individual guru for the benefit of the disciples. In the worship characteristic of passion-pursuing *bhakti* (*rāgānugā bhakti*), in which the godly, majestic aspect of divinity is subverted, one has a sweet vision of the guru as a dear girlfriend of Kṛṣṇa in the form called

---

[9] *Brahma-saṃhitā*, 5.45.

[10] Sanātana places Śiva fairly high in his hierarchy of recipients of Kṛṣṇa's grace in his *Bṛhad-bhāgavatāmṛta*. Śiva is above the earthly devotees (the pious Prayāga *brāhmaṇa* and the South Indian king), above Indra and Brahmā, but beneath Prahlāda and Hanumān. The entire third chapter of the first part of Sanātana's text is devoted to discussing Śiva's place in the hierarchy of *bhakti*. [Trans.]

[11] Actually, a more correct translation of the wording of the statement of this offense would be "thinking that all the names, qualities, and so forth of Śiva are different from those of Viṣṇu." In short, thinking of Śiva as different from Viṣṇu. That implies that Śiva is not independent of Viṣṇu, but goes somewhat further. "Not different" is a much stronger statement. The exact statement is:

> शिवस्य श्रीविष्णोर्य इह गुणनामादिसकलं।
> धिया भिन्नं पश्येत्स खलु हरिनामाहितकरः॥

[Trans.]

[12] Jīva, Bs, 286: य एव भगवानत्र व्यष्टिरूपतया भक्तावतारत्वेन श्रीगुरुरूपो वर्तते स एव तत्र समष्टिरूपतया स्ववामप्रदेशे साक्षादवतारत्वेनापि तद्रूपो वर्तते।

[13] Jīva, *Saṅkṣepa-vaiṣṇava-toṣaṇi* (Svt), on Bhāg. 10.80.34: गुरौ मदावेशेन साक्षान्मद्रूपतत्वात् मद्भक्तवररूपत्वाच्चेति भावः।

the *mañjarī*[14] form.[15] Not respecting such an affectionate spiritual parent is an offense to the Holy Name.

4. **Blasphemy of Scripture**. Blasphemy of *śruti* [the Veda], *smṛti* [the ritual and law texts], the Purāṇas [ancient histories and genealogies], and the scriptures that are based on them, or showing disrespect for them or lack of belief in them is one kind of offense to the Holy Name.[16]

5. **Hollow Praise**. Thinking that the passages in scripture that describe the greatness of the Holy Name are just hollow praise is an offense to the Holy Name.

6. **Thinking Fancifully with Respect to the Holy Name**. Considering undertaking some other means of practice in order to trivialize the greatness of the Holy Name is an offense to the Holy Name. If, however, out of mental anguish, the thought of some other means arises for the purpose of arriving at the goal faster, it is not an offense. But, if one's objective is making the greatness of the Holy Name secondary, it is an offense.[17]

7. **Sinning on the Strength of the Holy Name**. The power of the Holy Name delivers the highest goal of human life, the lotus-like feet of the Lord himself, the very solidification of eternal existence, consciousness and joy (*saccidānanda*). To use that unlimitedly powerful, supremely ambrosial Holy Name to acquire sensual pleasures like wealth, followers and so forth[18] is the greatest form of depravity toward the Holy Name. It is like using a *śālagrāma* stone[19]

---

[14] *Mañjarī* means "cluster of blossoms" or a "flower-bud." See the glossary for more details. [Trans.]

[15] Viśvanātha, *Gurvaṣṭaka*, 1:

साक्षाद्धरित्वेन समस्तशास्त्रै-
रुक्तस्तथा भाव्यत एव सद्भिः।
किन्तु प्रभोर्यः प्रिय एव तस्य
वन्दे गुरोः श्रीचरणारविन्दं।

[16] Viśvanātha, comm. on Bhāg., 10.33.49: शास्त्राविश्वासिनं नामापराधिनं

[17] Jīva, Ks. on Bhāg. 2.1.11: हरिनाम्नि कल्पनं तन्माहात्म्यगौणताकरणाय गत्यन्तरचिन्तनम्।

[18] "All sense objects are poisonous" (*viṣaya garalamaya*) says Śrī Narottama Dās (*Prema-bhakti-candrikā*).

[19] The *śālagrāma* stone is a sacred stone found in the rivers of Nepal and considered by Vaiṣṇavas to be a sacred form of Viṣṇu. They are thus worshipped as images of Viṣṇu. To use one to crack open a nut is to show total disregard for the stone's sacred meaning.

to crack open nuts.[20]

8. **Thinking Other Auspicious Actions are Equal to the Holy Name.** The Holy Name is the whole, the source (*aṅgī*). From this whole all the other limbs or forms of worship arise. Thinking that one of those parts is equal to the whole is an offense to the Holy Name. If one is able to overcome this offense, that is, if one seeks shelter in the Holy Name exclusively and with the greatest respect, thinking it the best of all, Lord Holy Name, who is affectionate to those who come to him for shelter, will protect one from the other nine offenses. This is his promise: "My devotee does not perish." (*na me bhaktaḥ praṇaśyati*) (*Bhagavad- gītā*, 9.31).[21]

9. **Instructing the Chanting of the Holy Name to the Faithless.**

10. **Not Feeling Pleasure on Hearing of the Greatness of the Holy Name.**

3.1 The Dangers of Wealth

Laghu: In the discussion of the seventh offense all sense objects were said to be sins on the evidence of the statements of Narottama Dāsa Ṭhākura. Still, some say: "The gold of a sense enjoyer is the cause of enjoyment. With that gold instead serve Mādhava (Kṛṣṇa). If it is used in service that sinful gold becomes Mādhava." Drawing this conclusion, such people continue to accumulate wealth. Is this idea correct?

Goswami: Look, money/wealth is the favorite residence of the Age of Kali. Although Mahārāja Parīkṣit gave Kali gambling, drinking, the killing of women and animals as places in which he might reside, with great fervor Kali begged for this place (money).[22] This place is the best

---

[20]Jīva, Ks. on Bhāg. 2.1.11: नाम्नो बलाद्यस्य हि पापबुद्धिरिति यद्यपि भगवन्नाम्नो बलेनापि कृतस्य पापस्य तेन नाम्ना क्षयस्तथापि येन नाम्नो बलेन परमपुरुषार्थरूपं सच्चिदानन्दसान्द्रं साक्षाच्छ्रीभगवच्चरणारविन्दं साधयितुं प्रवृत्तस्तेनैव परमघृणास्पदं पापं विषयं साधयतीति परमदौरात्म्यम्।

[21]Jīva, Ks. on Bhāg. 2.3.3: धर्मादिभिः साम्यमननमपि प्रमादोऽपराधो पाद्मे रामाष्टोत्तरशतनामस्तोत्रे विष्णोरेकैकनामापि सर्ववेदाधिकम्। See the further discussion of this offense in a later chapter.

[22]Bhāg., 1.17.39:

पुनश्च याचमानया जातरूपमदात्प्रभुः।
ततोऽनृतं मदं कामं रजो वैरञ्च पञ्चमम्॥

And again the Master [Mahārāja Parīkṣit] gave gold to him [Kali] who was

because wealth is very difficult for people to give up.[23] And, by getting that place, all the other [unwholesome] places will come by themselves. After receiving this place from Parīkṣit Mahārāja, Kali sat directly on top of money-wealth and made it his ancestral home. Now, who else can occupy it? Therefore, it is now seen, whether in the realm of material life or in the realm of religion, there is an uproar over money. One can give up everything, but the absorption in wealth cannot be given up. Is this difficult to give up or not? Therefore, it is said in the *Bhāgavata* that at the present time there is *dharma*, but it rests on fame and wealth.

In order to warn us about wealth, that hard-to-overcome source of harm, the most compassionate teacher of the world, Śrī Gaurahari, gave an instruction on this subject, directing it first to Raghunātha Dāsa, then to the rest of the world.

Śrī Raghunātha Gosvāmin accepted a little bit of money sent by his father only for the purpose of feeding, in his own room, his beloved lord, Śrī Gaurahari. For two years he invited him to eat. After that he stopped inviting him. Mahāprabhu then asked Svarūpa:

> Why has Raghu stopped inviting me?
> Svarūpa said: "He thought about it some:
> 'With the money of a materialist I invite him.
> He cannot be pleased with this. I know the Master's mind.'
> Thinking in that way he stopped inviting you."
> Hearing this, Mahāprabhu smiled and began to speak:
> "If one eats the food of a materialist,
> one's mind becomes unclean.
> If one's mind becomes unclean,
> one cannot remember Kṛṣṇa.
> The food of a materialist is a poluted invitation.[24]
> The giver and the receiver, both their minds become unclean."[25]

---

begging for it and from that (gold) also came untruth, intoxication, lust, violence, and enmity [as places for Kali to reside].

[23] Viśvanātha's comm. on Bhāg. 1.17.39: तस्मादेवं किमपि स्थानमहं प्राप्नुयां यन्नोकैर्दुस्त्यज्यम्

[24] An invitation tinged by the material quality of dimness. Dimness or *rajas* along with goodness (*sattva*, also clarity) and darkness (*tamas*) are the three material qualities or threads that run through material existence like threads through a cloth, according to the Hindu school of Sāṅkhya. [Trans.]

[25] Cc. Antya, 6.268-274:

raghu kene āmāy nimantraṇ chāḍi dilo

Now notice who is being called a materialist. Śrī Gaurahari has himself introduced us to Raghunātha's father and uncle:

> "Although they follow brahminical culture
> and are helpers of the *brāhmaṇa*,
> they are not pure Vaiṣṇavas;
> they are nearly Vaiṣṇavas."[26]

Many of the *brāhmaṇa* pandits of Navadvīpa were helped by the wealth of Raghunātha's father and uncle. Service of the *brāhmaṇa* is one of the sixty-four forms of *bhakti* — worshiping the Vaiṣṇava, the *brāhmaṇa*, cows and the *dhātrī*[27], *tulasī* (Sacred Basil), and *aśvattha* (fig) trees.[28] They had enough faith in the Vaiṣṇavas, too. Still, they were very wealthy and were busy with that wealth. Therefore, it is said of them that they were not pure Vaiṣṇava, only nearly Vaiṣṇava.

Okay, now think about this. In relation to such people Śrī Mahāprabhu has said: if you eat their food, your mind will become polluted and the Lord never accepts that.

We have to ask ourselves how much of this instruction of Mahāprabhu we are observing in our lives, especially when the entire world has fallen as a unit into the clutches of Kali. When the life of ordinary people is destroyed by an unnatural absorption in sense enjoyment — in one direction is a mountain of black money and in the other the deep, dark cave of poverty — such turmoil arises over a little food and something to wear. Any of the possessions that have fallen off the rotting, foul-smelling body of today's society into the hands of holy men are not just

---

svarūpa kahe mane kichu bicār karilo
biṣayīr drabyo lañā kari nimantraṇ
prasanna nā hoy ihāy, jāni prabhur man
eto bicāriyā nimantraṇ chāḍi dilo
śuni mahāprabhu hāsi bolite lāgilo
biṣayīr anno khāile malin hoy man
malin man haile nahe kṛṣṇa smaraṇ
biṣayīr anno hoy rājasa nimantraṇ
dātā bhoktā, duhār malin hoy man

[26] Cc, Antya, 6.196:

yadyapi brahmaṇyo kare brāhmaṇer sahāy
śuddha baiṣṇab nahe baiṣṇaber prāy

[27] This is the Emblic Myrobalan, also known as the *āmalaka* tree.
[28] Brs., 1.2.110.

ordinary poisons but are likely to be the very strongest and most dangerous poisons. What more can be said about this? Are these things to be thoughtlessly accepted and used in offerings to Gaura and Govinda, who are more dear to us than life itself? Didn't they reject offerings prepared with the wealth of Raghunātha's father and Duryodhana's offerings of all the four different types of sumptuous food arranged beautifully on a plate of pure gold?[29] If they reject such offerings, then whose nectar-like touch will neutralize their poisonous natures and turn them into the nature of Mādhava? Keeping their own natures (as poison) will they not instead bring about the destruction of the practitioner's life? Still, a person who worships Kṛṣṇa is very clever. Kali's cleverness will not work on him. Because he takes shelter in the Holy Name, Kali's web will miss him. Note Śrī Sanātana Gosvāmin's thought on this subject:

> The royal wealth of the Pāṇḍavas was envied even by the gods. That wealth was the result of Kṛṣṇa's grace and even though it was all offered to Kṛṣṇa, it could not create in King Yudhiṣṭhira even the slightest attachment for it. It was like the way fine clothes, garlands, sandalwood, and other such things are unable to make a man who is disturbed by hunger happy. That wealth was not able to make Yuddhiṣṭhira, whose mind was burning in the flames of love for Kṛṣṇa, happy.[30]

In his commentary Sanātana says:

> Why was the wealth of the Pāṇḍavas desired by the gods? In answer to this it is said: That wealth was free of all faults like being prone to loss and so forth, because it was the result of Kṛṣṇa's grace, not the result of their pious acts.
>
> Objection: Even if that is so, wealth, like the heat of fire, is by nature an abode of every fault and is thus harmful. Knowing this is knowing the truth.

[29] This is a traditional classification of types of food: those that are chewed, those that are sucked, those that are licked, and those that are drunk. [Trans.]

[30] Bb., 1.4.115-6:

> कृष्णप्रसादजनिताः कृष्ण एव समर्पिताः ।
> नाशकन् कामपि प्रीतिं राज्ञो जनयितुं क्वचित्॥
> कृष्णप्रेमाग्निदन्दह्यमानान्तःकरणस्य हि ।
> क्षुदग्निविकलस्येव वासःस्रक्चन्दनादयः॥

> Reply: Right, but since it is heard that if wealth is offered to the Lord it becomes immortal, it cannot have had any fault. Rather it was a veritable gold mine of good qualities. That is why in the verse it is said "offered to Kṛṣṇa."

For practitioners like us, this verse is especially worthy of consideration. Sanātana Gosvāmin in his commentary on this verse says: "offered completely to Kṛṣṇa, that is, without any desire for anything in return" (*kṛṣṇa eva samyaṅ niṣkāmatvādinā 'rpitāḥ*). Since Yudhiṣṭhira's wealth was offered completely, ie. without any desire, he (Sanātana) presents the meaning of the word *samarpita* in this way. If even a little desire or inclination remains, wealth offered to the Lord is not freed from its harmful nature.

Now one has to ask at what stage is one's mind completely free of desire or cleansed of its attachments? Up through the stage of strong attraction for Kṛṣṇa (*kṛṣṇa-rati,* also known as *bhāva*) a little attachment remains. Only on the stage of full blown love (*preman*) is the mind completely free of desire. Therefore, it appears that only devotees who have love are able to turn poisonous sense-objects (wealth) into nectar (immortality) — they have the power to cause sense objects to leave behind their faulty natures and take on beneficial ones. But the difficulty is that although they have that power, for those on that stage there is no time to turn around and glance in any other direction. They run about like lunatics asking "where can I find Vrajendranandana (the Son of the King of Vraja, ie., Kṛṣṇa)?" in order to try to bring some peace to their hearts which are burning with love for Kṛṣṇa.

On this topic one should consider one more thing. Becoming dear to Kṛṣṇa is achieved by giving up sense enjoyments, not accepting them. Therefore, in the *Bhāgavata* Kṛṣṇa tells Uddhava:

> Uddhava, my son Brahmā, my alter-ego Śaṅkara, even my most intimate Lakṣmī are not as dear to me as you, my devotee, is. This is because my devotees have to give up everything and become possessionless in order to come to me. The others, though, don't have to give up anything; they are by nature close to me.[31]

From this, one can understand that it is by renunciation that one becomes dear to the Lord, not by receiving.

[31] Bhāg., 11.14.15-16.

Chapter 4

Saṅkīrtana in Single-form Practice

Laghu: In the *Bhakti-rasāmṛta-sindhu* sixty-four forms of *bhakti* are described.[1] Are we to practice all of them, or any one of them? By which of them are we best be able to achieve our goal?

Goswami: The answer to that can be found in one of Śrī Rūpa's verses from that same *Bhakti-rasāmṛta-sindhu*:

> That *bhakti,* either in one main form or in many forms, in accordance with one's own inner inclination (*vāsanā*), executed with unwavering steadiness brings accomplishment.[2]

Viśvanātha's commentary on this is:

> Performing one of the forms from among the nine types of *bhakti* (hearing, *kīrtana,* and so forth) as one's main practice and performing as secondary practices other required forms,

---

[1]See Rūpa Gosvāmin's Brs, First Section, Chapter Two.
[2]Brs., 1.2.264:

सा भक्तिरेकमुख्याङ्गाश्रितानेकाङ्गिकाथवा।
स्ववासनानुसारेण निष्ठातः सिद्धिकृद्भवेत्॥

> such as taking shelter at the feet of a guru, observing *Ekādaśī*,[3] and so forth is called single-form *bhakti*. Performing several of the nine forms and the other required forms is called multi-form *bhakti*. If, according to one's own inclinations, one gains firmness in either single- or multi-form *bhakti*, one achieves success.[4]

The *Caitanya-caritāmṛta* says: "Some practice single-form and some multi-form. When one becomes fixed in it, the wave of love arises."[5]

Laghu: If that is so, then in single-form worship can we choose any one of those forms among hearing, *kīrtana*, remembering, and so forth, as our main focus?

Goswami: No you cannot. There is a variation in *dharma* according to place, time, and person. In the Age of Kali the *dharma* of the age is *kīrtana*, repetition or chanting of the Holy Names. That should be the main form, whether in single-form or multi-form *bhakti*. That is the instruction of scripture. Take, for instance: "the wise worship by sacrifices that mostly consist of *saṅkīrtana*" (*yajñaiḥ saṅkīrtanaprāyair yajanti hi sumedhasaḥ*).[6] And in the *Caitanya-caritāmṛta* it is said:

> In the age of Kali is the *dharma*
> *saṅkīrtana* of Kṛṣṇa's names.
> They worship him by *saṅkīrtana*-sacrifice,
> those who are wise; the rest by Kali fall to their demise."[7]

Moreover, in Rūpa's verse he discusses forms (parts, *aṅga*), not the whole. The Holy Name is at one and the same time both the whole and

---

[3]The eleventh day of the full moon and new moon cycles. This is a fast day for Vaiṣṇava practitioners.

[4]Viśvanātha on Brs., 1.2.264: श्रवणकीर्तनादिनां मध्ये मुख्यतया क्रियमाणमेकमङ्गं यस्याः सा। तथा चान्यानि तु गौणतया क्रियमाणानीति लभ्यते। आश्रितान्यनेकाङ्गानि यस्याः सा। अत्र कल्पद्रुयमेव श्रेष्ठमित्याह स्ववासनेति॥

[5]Cc., Madhya, 22.76: *ek aṅga sādhe, keho sādhe bahu aṅga, niṣṭhā haile upajaye premer taraṅga*

[6]Bhāg. 11.5.32 and Viśvanātha's comm.: "those who are wise [worship] by a predominance of *saṅkīrtana* ... " सङ्कीर्तनप्रधानैर्यै सुमेधसः

[7]Cc., Madhya, 11.87-8:

> *kalikāle dharma kṛṣṇanāma saṅkīrtan,*
> *saṅkīrtan yajñe tānre kore ārādhan,*
> *sei to sumedhā ār kalihato jan.*

the part. The parts belong to the whole — as a tree is the whole and the leaves, flowers, and fruit are its parts [or forms]. Hearing, *kīrtana*, and all the others are forms of *bhakti*; they must have some whole or source. That whole is the Lord Holy Name. From the whole, Lord Holy Name, which is like a seed, all the other forms of worship come forth.[8] One Name of Kṛṣṇa is the whole (or seed) and that is expanded into many branches in the form of *kīrtana* of the Holy Names, just as from one seed, which is the single cause, comes a tree and from that tree come hundreds and thousands of seeds.

In the *Caitanya-caritāmṛta* it is said that the five last forms of *bhakti* headed by association with the holy are the best and "among those the best of all is *saṅkīrtana* of the Holy Names."[9] Again, in another place it is said: in exhilaration the Master said: "listen, Svarūpa and Rāma Rāya, in the Age of Kali *kīrtana* of the Holy Names is the highest way."[10] It is the highest way — that is, it is the way of ways. In other words, the other forms of *bhakti* are causes of love and the cause of those causes is the seed, the whole, *saṅkīrtana* of the Holy Names. Without the seed the tree is just imaginary — therefore, the highest practice and *dharma* of the age of Kali, the seed, this *saṅkīrtana* of the Holy Names, cannot be excluded under any condition: "In Kali there is no other, there is no other, there is no other way," (*kalau nāstyeva nāstyeva nāstyeva gatiranyathā*). Therefore, if someone wants to gain perfection in the Age of Kali by only one form, he must take up that independent and singular whole, the Holy Name. That one complete whole, the Holy Name, will manifest in many branch Holy Names and, immersed in the joy of *kīrtana* of the Holy Names, the devotee will say: "May I have thousands and thousands of births so that I may relish the Names of the dark-skinned one (Kṛṣṇa)."[11]

The Holy Name is a powerful thing. Since he has attained such a

---

[8]The author cites in his footnote three passages in which the Holy Name is referred to as the "seed" of *bhakti* practice. Cc., Antya, 20.10: [From *saṅkīrtana*] arise all forms of *bhakti* practice (*sarva-bhakti-sādhan udgama*); Cc. Ādi 8.26: [Then I know that there is massive offense,] since through the seed of the Name of Kṛṣṇa nothing germinates, (*kṛṣṇa-nāma bīj tāhe nā hoy aṅkur*); and in a verse quoted in Śrī Rūpa Gosvāmin's *Padyāvalī*, 19: [The Name of Kṛṣṇa is] the seed of the tree of *dharma*, (*bījaṃ dharma-drumasya*). [Trans.]

[9]The five forms of *bhakti* that are listed last in Rūpa's list of 64 forms are considered the best and they are: worshipping images of Kṛṣṇa, listening to the *Bhāgavata Purāṇa*, associating with devotees with similar moods, *saṅkīrtana* of the Names of Kṛṣṇa and living in the area around the ancient town of Mathurā. Cc., Antya, 4.66: *tār madhye sarvaśreṣṭha nām saṅkīrtan*.

[10]Cc., Antya, 20.7: *harṣe kahe prabhu śon svarūp rām rāy, nāmasaṅkīrtan kalau parama upāy*

[11]So in fact says Īśvarapurī, disciple of Mādhavendra Purī and guru of Śrī Caitanya: श्यामलधामनामजुषतां जम्नास्तु लक्षावधि

powerful thing the devotee is complete. He doesn't feel the need for anything else. That said, he still does not neglect the other forms of *bhakti*. Therefore, look at the example given in the *Caitanya-caritāmṛta* of someone who has achieved success by only one form — Vaiyāsaki, the son of Vyāsa, Śrī Śukadeva — and that too in the form of *kīrtana*. Śrī Śukadeva praised the Holy Name by *kīrtana* of the *Śrīmad Bhāgavata*, the *purāṇa* of the Holy Name, in the assembly of Mahārāja Parīkṣit.

In this Age of Kali, even without practicing remembering (*smaraṇa*)[12] and the rest of the forms of practical *bhakti*, every success can be achieved. In other words by the *saṅkīrtana* of the Holy Names alone, independent of any other form, one can develop the love found in Vraja, which is the highest aim of all living beings, and enter into the sacred bowers as a *mañjarī*. On this topic, the evidence comes from the words of Śrī Sanātana Gosvāmin:

> Among the many different types of praising (*kīrtana*) Kṛṣṇa, praising with his Holy Names is the best. This is so because the *kīrtana* of his Holy Names is quickly able to produce the treasure of divine love (*preman*). Therefore, the learned have determined that it is the best among all the forms of *bhakti*.[13]

To paraphrase Sanātana's commentary, it is said previously, in the verse beginning "We consider ... " (*manyāmahe*) (2.3.148), that *kīrtana* is better than remembering (*smaraṇa*). Now, among all the different types of *kīrtana*, like reciting from the Vedas and Purāṇas, telling stories about Kṛṣṇa, reciting the Names, describing his forms, qualities, and sports, singing songs and offering prayers, repetition of the Holy Names is the main form. Why is it the main form? Because *kīrtana* of the Holy Names, without the help of remembering and so forth, is able quickly and by itself to cause the treasure of love for Kṛṣṇa to appear. For this reason it is even better than meditation. Therefore, *kīrtana* of the Names of Kṛṣṇa

[12]The general definition of remembering (*smaraṇa*) is drawing the mind away from all other things and causing it to enter directly into, or become absorbed in, Kṛṣṇa. सर्वतो मन आकृष्य मय्यद्धावेश्यते यथा. This is from Jīva's Bs, 275 in which he quotes Bhāg. 11.13.14.

[13]Bb., 2.3.158:

कृष्णस्य नानाविधकीर्तनेषु
तन्नामकीर्तनमेव मुक्यम्।
तत्प्रेमसम्पज्जनने स्वयं द्राक्
शक्तं ततः श्रेष्ठतमं मतं तत्॥

is the best of all. This is the opinion of all the saintly ones and it is my (Sanātana's) opinion, too.[14]

Laghu: This treasure of love that you just spoke of, is it duty-motivated (*vaidhī*) love or passion-pursuing (*rāgānugā*) love?

Goswami: The answer to that question will be found in many places if one studies carefully the *Bṛhad-bhāgavatāmṛta* (Great Ambrosia of Matters Related to the Lord) of Śrī Sanātana Gosvāmin. Only a brief discussion will be given here. In the previously cited verse (2.3.158), it is granted that one attains love by *kīrtana* of the names of Rādhā and Kṛṣṇa without depending on remembering and the rest. If that is so then the conclusion can be easily drawn from that that if someone sits on the bank of Rādhākuṇḍa and, without depending on any other practice, cries out "Rādhā! Rādhā!" and knows nothing other than that, most compassionate Rādhā will certainly give that person a place at her feet and make the person successful. She will not send such a person to Lakṣmī in Vaikuṇṭha with duty-motivated *bhakti*.

Therefore, after the previously mentioned verse (2.3.158), in verse 163, *kīrtana* and remembering are again compared and *kīrtana* of the Holy Names is said to be better than remembering. In the commentary on that verse the cause of *kīrtana*'s being better than remembering is stated: it is able to bestow love that has reached the highest limit of all. From this one clearly understands that what remembering independently cannot do, *kīrtana* of the Holy Names can do — bestow the service of Rādhā — without depending on anything else. Therefore, it is the best.

Moreover, in another verse of the *Bṛhad-bhāgavatāmṛta* (2.1.21) an interesting question is raised. What place will they attain who, desiring to serve Rādhā, do *kīrtana* of the Names of the Enjoyer of the Rāsa Dance (Kṛṣṇa) without depending on any of the other forms of practice or on any of the other goals like Vaikuṇṭha?

In the commentary on this verse, the author has raised the question in an even sweeter way: "Out of all of the various goals like going to Vaikuṇṭha and so forth and out of all the various methods like hear-

[14]Sanātana, comm. on Bb. 2.3.158: तत्र च श्रीभगवन्नामसङ्कीर्तनमेव सेव्यमित्याशयेनाहुः कृष्ण-स्येति। नानाविधेषु वेदपुराणादिपाठकथागीतस्तुत्यादिभेदेन बहुप्रकारेषु कीर्तनेषु मध्ये तस्य कृष्णस्य नामकीर्तनमेव मुख्यम्। कुतः द्रागविलम्बेनैव तस्मिन् कृष्णे प्रेमसम्पदो जनने आविर्भावणे स्वयमनन्यैरपेक्ष्येणैव शक्तं समर्थम्। ततस्तस्माद्धेतोर्ध्यानादिति वा। तच्छ्रीकृष्णनामसङ्कीर्तननेव श्रेष्ठतमं मतं सद्भिरस्माभिर्वा।

ing, *kīrtana*, remembering and so forth, for those who want only to enter the service of Rādhā without depending on anything else, what is the method most efficacious in achieving that highest of goals? **That method is the *saṅkīrtana* of the Holy Names of Kṛṣṇa, the relisher of the Rāsa dance (*rāsa-rasika*).**[15] The place attained by one who does *kīrtana* of the names of Rāsa-rasika Kṛṣṇa is identified in a later verse (2.1.24): "that place, higher than Vaikuṇṭha, is the highest limit of sweetness, Śrī Vṛndāvana — the center of passionate *bhakti*."[16]

Therefore, according to the discussion above, there is a distinction in the places one may achieve. From repetition of the holy names of Kṛṣṇa, the enjoyer of the Rāsa dance, by itself without dependence on any other process, one not only gets passion-based *bhakti*, but within it one gets the best thing of all, the very service of Rādhā herself. There is no higher achievement for a living being. Those who, sitting on the banks of Rādhākuṇḍa, call out "Rādhā, Rādhā!" all day and night, drenching themselves in tears, not depending on any other practice like remembering and so forth, most compassionate Rādhā will take as her own servants and will keep them there on the bank of Rādhākuṇḍa. She will not give them duty-motivated *bhakti* and send them off to Vaikuṇṭha. What more need be said?

Moreover, Śrī Sanātana has said in his commentary on the verse beginning "Victory, victory to the joyful form of the Name of Murāri" (*jayati jayati nāmānandarūpaṃ murāreḥ*) (Bb, 1.1.9): "However, *kīrtana* of the Holy Names of Kṛṣṇa is for me, who does not depend on any other process like meditation and so forth, the complete and true result. That is, it is the highest goal in the form of passion-pursuing love that has reached its absolutely highest limit. It is the highest ambrosia, my very life and only adornment. This alone, the *kīrtana* of the Holy Names, is my greatest support and the bringer of all (*sarva*) grace. In other words, taking me by the hand it leads me to Rādhā's bower in Vṛndāvana."[17]

The word "all" extends to everything; it is not bound by any limits. In the Sanskrit lexicon, the *Amara-koṣa*, the meaning of the word "all"

---

[15] This sentence is in boldface in the original.

[16] Bb., 2.1.24: तदर्थमुचितं स्थानमेकं वैकुण्ठतः परम्।

[17] Sanātana says nothing about being taken by the hand and led to Rādhā's bower in his commentary. This is a fanciful addition of the author as will be made clear from the following paragraph. [Trans.] Sanātana's actual words are: मम तु तत्तत्सर्वनिरपेक्षस्य तदेवैकमखिलं सत्फलमित्याह यदिति। अमृतं निर्वाणसुखं परमामृतं मुक्तिसुखाधिकाधिकवैकुण्ठसुखं किंवा मधुरमधुरमित्यर्थः। परममित्यनुवर्तत एव परमं जीवनं परमं भूषणञ्च तदेकमेव मम परमापेक्ष्यं सर्वशोभासम्पादकञ्चेति दिक्।

(*sarva*) is given as: full, unbroken, complete and so forth. Therefore, here, the words "all grace" mean that which is the highest of all within the love whose essential nature is erotic.[18] That is to be understood as the attainment of service to Rādhā in her bower and the relishing of the feelings in her heart. That is the highest achievement for the living being.

On this topic, there is one other subject that is worthy of pursuit. From the books of the followers of Śrī Gaura we learn that after Śrī Gaura's appearance in the world a [new] *rasa* will remain, passion-pursuing *bhakti-rasa*, which is the real treasure of the realm of immense sweetness, Vṛndāvana. Duty-born *bhakti* was given, as if shaken out of the bag last, before the appearance of Śrī Gaura, by the Alvars of the South — like the preparations of court officials before the coming of the great emperor.

Therefore, Prabodhānanda Sarasvatī in his *Caitanya-candrāmṛta* (Ambrosia of the Moon of Caitanya) and Ānandi in his commentary on that verse say:

> When moon-like Caitanya revealed the path of *bhakti-yoga* [*rāgānuga-bhakti*] in the world, everyone gave up their various other practices and became absorbed in the rapture (*rasa*) of passionate *bhakti*. No other form of sacred rapture (*bhakti-rasa*) remained.[19]

That was the situation when Śrī Gaura was manifest. So that the same situation would remain after his disappearance, Gaurahari gave a blessing to the world of the future before his departure. In answer to Śrī Advaita Prabhu's prayer he said:

---

[18]In Caitanya Vaiṣṇava theology though each of the five main forms of attraction to Kṛṣṇa (*kṛṣṇa-rati*) is appealing to some people on the basis of their internal inclinations, the erotic form, also called sweetnesss or the blazing one, is considered the most flavorful and therefore the highest. See Rūpa in his Brs, 2.5.38.

[19]Prabodhānanda Sarasvatī, *Caitanya-candrāmṛta* (Cca), 10.113:

> स्त्रीपुत्रादिकथां जुहुर्विषयिणः शास्त्रप्रवादं बुधा
> योगीन्द्रा विजुहुर्मरुन्नियमजक्लेशं तपस्तापसाः।
> ज्ञानाभ्यासविधिं जहुश्च यतयश्चैतन्यचन्द्रे परां
> आविष्कुर्वति भक्तियोगपदवीं नैवान्य आसीद्रसः॥

and Ānandi: चैतन्यचन्द्रे परां निगूढप्रेमलक्षणानुभाविकां भक्तियोगस्य पदवीं रागानुगीयमार्गमाविष्कुर्वति।

> Among those practicing duty-born *bhakti*, some feel at home as servants and some as friends and among those some are for Rādhā and Mādhava and some for the Lord of Dvārakā. Yet others are devoted to other descents like Rāma, Nṛsiṃha, and the others. I will attract them all to me and bind them by the ropes of love. I will give all of them the feelings of the *bhakti* of Vṛndāvana.[20]

The blessing of that savior of the Age of Kali, most compassionate Gaurahari, can never be ineffective. This is the highest truth. This is the greatest reassurance for living beings who are stricken by the age of Kali. That which Brahmā, Śiva, and the rest of the gods wish for, but which is never given them, love at its highest culmination, we will receive easily through *kīrtana* of the Holy Names.

Laghu: There is a statement of Śrī Narottama Dāsa Ṭhākura: "What one meditates on (ie., remembers) in practice one will achieve in the perfected body. On the path of passion, that is the way."[21] Isn't that a contradiction to these teachings of Sanātana and the other Gosvāmins then? How can one reconcile them?

Goswami: It is a contradiction merely fabricated in your mind. Listen, Śrī Rūpa in his *Bhakti-rasāmṛta-sindhu* and later Kṛṣṇadāsa Kavirāja in the *Caitanya-caritāmṛta* have written: "Some practice one form; some practice many. If one becomes unwavering in practice, the wave of love will arise. By one form many devotees have reached success."[22] Basically, the context is this: Here two separate channels of worship (*bhajana*) are mentioned, each of which has the same potency to bestow love. Śrī

---

[20] Prabodhānanda Sarasvatī, Cca., 10.74:

> दास्ये केचन प्रणयिनः सख्ये त एवोभये
> राधामाधवनिष्ठया कतिपये श्रीद्वारकाधीशितुः।
> सख्यादावुभयत्र केचन परे ये वावतारान्तरे
> मय्याबद्धहृदोऽखिलान् वितनैव वृन्दावनासङ्गिनः॥

[21] Narottama Dāsa Ṭhākura, *Prema-bhakti-candrikā*, 5:

> *sādhane bhābibe yāhā,*
> *siddha dehe pābe tāhā,*
> *rāgapathe ei se upāy*

[22] Cc., Madhya, 22.76-7: *ek aṅge sādhe keha, keha sādhe bahu aṅga. niṣṭhā haile upajaye premer taraṅga. ek aṅge siddhi pāilo bahubhaktagaṇa.*

Narottama Dāsa described the second channel — the form of remembering in which *kīrtana* of the Holy Names is dominant. This applies to the phrase "what one meditates on in practice one will achieve in perfection," here. He has not mentioned the first channel. The first channel that he does not mention should not be brought in for comparision.

If someone says that Rāma can lift five *maund*,[23] does it lead to the conclusion that Lakṣmaṇa cannot? It doesn't. If one wanted to convey *that* meaning one would have to say something like: "Only Rāma can lift five *maund*, no one else."[24] Since Narottama Dāsa Ṭhākur has not said that, worrying about a contradiction is useless, just a figment of your imagination.

Laghu: Is a practitioner of the single form, *kīrtana* of the Holy Names, then cheated out of remembering the holy sports or out of performing mental service to Rādhā and Govinda when the divine couple is intoxicated by their own joyful sports?

Goswami: No, he is not cheated out of anything. By the mercy of Lord Holy Name he will easily remember the holy sports and attain mental service and the rest — not in the form of means or method of cultivation (*sādhana*), but in the form of end or ultimate realization (*sādhya*).

The beginning of *vaidhī-bhakti* is the regulation of scripture. And the starting point of *rāga-bhakti* is strong desire. That strong desire arises from the hearing and *kīrtana* of the super sweet Names of Kṛṣṇa pertaining to Gokula and from the hearing and *kīrtana* of the storehouse of sweetness, the *Purāṇa* of the Holy Names, the *Bhāgavata Purāṇa*.

Therefore, whether one chants, without depending on anything else, the Holy Names of Gokula, which is the very seed of everything, as a single-form, or whether one practices many forms — what is produced will be passionate *bhakti*, whose very life is remembering. How can one think that by planting the seed of a Langra mango one will get some other kind of mango? Consequently, let the practitioner practice remembering or not practice it, remembering will come and take hold of him in due time. This taking hold can happen in the stage of practice or in the stage of accomplishment — if it grips one in the stage of practice then the flow of practice will be multi-formed; if it grips one in the stage

---

[23] A *maund* is a measure of weight in India that equals in different localities from 25 to 82 lbs. Five *maund* thus equals up to 410 lbs.

[24] As Śrī Jīva says in the *Krama-sandarbha* on Bhāg. 5.6.18: "Because it is not said 'at all' (*karhicidapi*) and because [words formed from] *cit* and *cana* do not apply to all cases ..." कर्हिचिदपीत्यनुक्तत्वाद् असाकल्ये तु चिच्चनावित्यमरकोषाच्च

of accomplishment (*sādhya*) practice will be single-formed. The mercy of Lord Holy Name is independent with regard to the time a person is swept up by remembrance. But a single-form practitioner does not have less of the astonishment of relishing — rather one's relishing increases day by day and approaches the highest stage. This is the quality of coming into contact with Lord Holy Name whose very nature is the highest ambrosia: *no jāne janitā kiyadbhiramṛtaiḥ kṛṣṇeti varṇadvayī*, "I don't know of how much nectar these two syllables 'kṛṣ na' are made."[25]

In our previous discussion, too, it was said that the love that arises as a result of *kīrtana* of the Holy Names is the love that is the source of the elevated, inflamed rasa (*unnata-ujjvala-rasa*), the best among the types of passionate love known in Vraja. That love's essential characteristic is "intense thirst for the beloved" called *rāga*. Its marginal characteristic is "absorption in the beloved."[26] That thirst is the powerful desire to make one's beloved happy by serving him according to one's deep feelings. Its effects are manifested in remembering the names, forms, qualities, sports and so forth of one's beloved and in absorption in mental service.

Therefore, it appears that those who have reached the goal by the single form of *kīrtana* of the Holy Names, while not taking up remembering during the period of cultivation, do become absorbed in the divine sports at the time of their accomplishment. In other words, remembering comes and grabs hold of them on its own — like some ghost which, even though unwanted, comes and settles down on one's shoulders, refusing to leave. In that way, the appearance [of the sport] comes and settles down on one and even if one wishes to leave it behind one cannot. This they call absorption (*āviṣṭatā* or *tanmayatā*) in the beloved.

Therefore, take note. Even though remembering may not be present as a form of practice, remembering of the divine sports is ever present on the level of accomplishment for the practitioner of a single form of *bhakti*.

At that stage, meditation and *kīrtana* go hand-in-hand. Śrī Sanātana Gosvāmin has described that stage in his *Bṛhad-bhāgavatāmṛta*:

> From *kīrtana* the joy of meditation is increased and from meditation the sweet joy of *kīrtana* is increased. We, indeed, think both meditation and repetition are to be practiced.[27]

---

[25] Rūpa, *Vidagdha-mādhava* (Vm), 1.15.

[26] *Caitanya-caritāmṛta*, Madhya, 22.86.

[27] Sanātana, Bb., 2.3.153:

This coming of remembering in the stage of accomplishment is the grace of Lord Holy Name. In this matter there is no room for argument — "in an inconceivable matter the application of logic is not fitting."[28] This single-form *bhakti* is not in any way inferior to many-formed *bhakti* — the two are equally the best.[29]

Laghu: Some, pushing forward Sanātana's verse beginning with "Among the many different types of *kīrtana* of Kṛṣṇa ... " (*kṛṣṇasya nānāvidha ...*),[30] want to belittle or disparage the remembering form of *bhakti*. Is that justified?

Goswami: Drawing that sort of conclusion from Śrī Sanātana's verse is bizarre indeed. The Names and the Named are not different. Just as the Named has names, forms, qualities, and activities, the Names, too, have the Named's forms, qualities, and activities. The Names, the very embodiment of unfragmented *rasa*, have boundless power like the Named; in compassion and magnanimity the Names are even greater than the Named. Keeping that magnaminity, compassion and power of the Names as his focus, Sanātana composed that verse. The test of the strength of an elephant is in uprooting *śāla* trees, not in uprooting banana trees.

Our general method of worship is found in the commentary on Sanātana's *Bṛhad-bhāgavatāmṛta*, verse 2.3.153: "But we think that both meditation and repetition are to be practiced."[31]

Even though, by the independent wish of Lord Holy Name, a single-form practitioner who is inspired by the verse, "Among the many different types of *kīrtana* ... ," who is attracted by the Holy Names, and who is a great enjoyer of *rasa* is rarely found, one *can* become one. Lord Holy Name will give that person the greatest treasure of the *rasa* of love and taking him by the hand will bring him to Rādhā's bower in the manner of one perfected by mercy. This is the Gosvāmin's intention in that verse; this is his heart's intent; he does not intend to reject remembering. If one disrespects the practice of remembering today, one would be disrespect-

---

सङ्कीर्तनाद्ध्यानसुखं विवर्धते।
ध्यानाच्च सङ्कीर्तनमाधुरीसुखम्।

The commentary says: "But we think both meditation and *saṅkīrtana* are to be performed," वयं तु ध्यानं सङ्कीर्तनञ्च द्वयमेव सेव्यं मन्यामहे.

[28] *Mahābhārata*, Bhīṣma, 5: अचिन्त्या खलु ये भावा: and so forth.

[29] Śrī Viśvanātha Cakravartin's comm. on Brs., 1.2.264: अत्र कल्पद्वयमेव श्रेष्ठम्

[30] Bb., 2.3.158.

[31] Comm. on Bb., 2.3.153: वयं तु ध्यानं सङ्कीर्तनं च द्वयमेव सेव्यं मन्यामहे

ing the memory of the previous teachers. Consequently, that would be the offense of disregarding the teacher.

Śrī Gaurahari along with his companions descended into this world in order to spread passion-pursuing *bhakti* the main form of which is remembering. Even though the people of the world could recognize passionate love in Kṛṣṇa's Vraja sports they could not attain it. To bestow it on the people of the world Gaura came.[32] Its practices are said to be: "in the external body of the practitioner one practices hearing, repeating (*kīrtana*), and so forth; and in the mind one visualizes one's own perfected body and day and night serves Kṛṣṇa in Vraja."[33] We have to perform this *bhakti* on the path of passion according to the gradual path indicated by the one who brought it (Śrī Gaura) and his followers (the Gosvāmin), not according to our own whims.

No one will disagree that mangoes are a very sweet fruit. Still, there can be different opinions concerning the way to acquire them. Foolish people will stare at the sweet fruit and cry insincere tears and smart people will at an opportune moment search for a seed, plant it in the ground, and carefully water it. This is the difference. The first group's essence is insincere tears and the second group in time will have the good fortune of tasting mangoes. Remembering is not of the nature of a seed, however; it is produced from a seed. "All *bhakti* has its source in practice."[34] What is that seed? The *Caitanya-caritāmṛta* uncovers that seed for us while describing the limitless power of the Holy Name:

> One name of Kṛṣṇa destroys all sin
> and manifests *bhakti*, the cause of love.[35]

and

---

[32]Cc., Ādi, 4.34:

> *premaras niryās karite āsvādan*
> *rāgamārga bhakti loke karite pracāraṇ*

"To cause the tasting of the juice of the *rasa* of love; to spread in the world the *bhakti* of the path of passion."

[33]Cc., Madhya, 22.89-90.

[34]Cc., Antya, 20.13.

[35]Cc., Ādi, 8.26:

> *ek kṛṣṇanāme kare sarvapāpa nāś*
> *premer kāraṇ bhakti karen prakāś*

> If one repeats that name of Kṛṣṇa many times,
> and if love still does not arise and tears don't flow,
> then I'm sure, there is a lot of offense.
> The seed, the name of Kṛṣṇa, has not sprouted.[36]

Moreover, in the statement: "the seed of the tree of *dharma*" (*bījaṃ dharmadrumasya*), in verse nineteen in Rūpa's collection of poetry, the *Padyāvalī* (String of Poems), this same seed is discovered as well. Therefore, from the aforementioned evidence it is clearly shown that in passion-pursuing *bhakti* repeating the names of Kṛṣṇa is the seed.

After performing continually the *kīrtana* of the names of Kṛṣṇa, when mental purity arises, then remembering too will arise in due course. Therefore, Śrī Jīva has said: "If the internal instrument (the mind) is pure, then without giving up *kīrtana* of the Holy Names one should engage in remembering."[37]

Now you have been able to understand that just as one should not disregard the remembering form of *bhakti*, since it is an offense, so too one should not disrespect the words of the Gosvāmins or take them out of context. That is the offense of disrespect of the guru. Moreover, it is altogether a mistake to remember the private [erotic] sports while in the grip of harmful inclinations or habits (*anartha*). "It is not fitting for those whose senses are in a condition of sexual arousal or who have the feelings like those of parents and servants to reflect on the private sports of Rādhā and Kṛṣṇa, since it contradicts their own moods."[38]

Laghu: Very well then, is there any need for a practitioner of single-form *bhakti* to take shelter at the feet of a guru, to receive initiation, to observe *Ekādaśī* and so forth? And if there is a need for him to accept all those other forms, how can one call his form of practice single?

Goswami: Perviously it was said the "one" means one from among the nine main forms of *bhakti* headed by hearing. If one mixes in another of those main forms it is no longer single-form *bhakti*. The twenty

[36]Cc., 1.8.29-30:

> *hena kṛṣṇanāma yadi lay bahubār*
> *tabu yadi prema nahe nahe aśru dhār*
> *tabe jāni aparādha tāhāte pracur*
> *kṛṣṇanāma bīj tāhe nā hay aṅkur*

[37]Jīva, Ks., 7.5.25: शुद्धान्तःकरणश्चेन्नामकीर्तनापरित्यागेन स्मरणं कुर्यात्

[38]Jīva, Bs., 339: रहस्यलीला तु पौरुषविकारवदिन्द्रियैः पितृपुत्रदासभावैश्च नोपास्या स्वीयभाव-विरोधात्. This is Śrī Jīva's comment on the closing verse of the description of the Rāsa-līlā in the *Bhāgavata Purāṇa*.

forms, however, from "taking shelter at the feet of a guru" to "not giving distress to the mind of any living being"[39] are like the gateway into the realm of *bhakti*.[40] If one wants to enter into the realm of *bhakti* one has to enter by that gateway. There is no other way. Even though one enters through that gateway, since the main form which the devotee adopts captures his complete attention, he hardly notices the gateway. These other forms that are the gateway become secondary therefore.[41] In this way there is no loss of the singleness of form.

---

[39] The twenty are: (1) shelter at the feet of a guru, (2) initiation, (3) service of the guru, (4) inquiry into true law (*dharma*), (5) following the path of the good, (6) giving up personal enjoyment out of affection for Kṛṣṇa, (7) living in a sacred place of Kṛṣṇa, (8) accepting only what one needs, (9) fasting on Ekādaśī, (10) honoring *dhatrī*, fig trees, cattle, *brāhmaṇa*, and Vaiṣṇava, (11) avoiding offenses in service and to the Names, (12) rejecting association with non-Vaiṣṇava, (13) not taking on many disciples, (14) not studying or cultivating many books or arts, (15) being equal in loss and gain, (16) not being dominated by sadness, (17) not calumniating other gods or scripture, (18) not calumniating Viṣṇu or Vaiṣṇavas, (19) not listening to obscene talk, and (20) not giving distress to any living being.

[40] Rūpa Gosvāmin, Brs., 1.2.83:

अस्यास्तत्र प्रवेशाय द्वारत्वेऽप्यङ्गविंशतः।
त्रयं प्रधानमेवोक्तं गुरुपादाश्रयादिकम्॥

[41] Viśvanātha Cakravartin's comm. on Brs, 1.2.264: तथा चान्याङ्गानि तु गौणतया क्रियमानानीति लभ्यते

Chapter 5

Faith and Initiation

Laghu: Okay, you have said that *kīrtana* of the Holy Names itself is able to bestow love without dependence on anything else. Here a question arises then: Isn't there any dependence on faith (*śraddhā*)?

Goswami: The Name of Kṛṣṇa, who is the cause of all causes, who is capable of accomplishing everything, who is possessed of limitless power — on what must it depend? Where is there room for any increase in that which is eternally full? What indeed can cause it to increase? Still, whether it depends on another or not, it is dependent on its own happiness or lack thereof. When the Name is happy, it dances in its own joy. Then it can create a flood of love. Again, when the Name is unhappy — it sits with its head bent and is not able to produce a single drop. The most compassionate Lord Holy Name is happy in all instances except in the case of an offense. Where there is an offense He is not pleased or happy. In that condition there is a dependence on faith or respect. If one takes Him to one's chest with faith or respect His unhappiness is cut away and His compassionate hand reaches out. "A person with faith is qualified for *bhakti*."[1] "When, by some chance association with great ones and their granting of grace, a person's good fortune arises and that person develops faith in discussions of my names and such, then that person's *bhakti* becomes complete."[2]

On this topic Śrī Jīva's discussion in his *Krama-sandarbha* is particu-

[1]Cc, Madhya, 22.38.

[2]Bhāg., 11.20.8: यदृच्छया मत्कथादौ जातश्रद्धस्तु यः पुमान्.

larly valuable:[3]

> The meaning of the word 'faith' here is trust (*viśvāsa*), because due to one's trust in the various discussions of the Lord one becomes detached from other actions. Complete engagement in those discussions is needed. Without faith such complete engagement internally and externally does not happen. This complete engagement then depends on faith — without faith, unmixed *bhakti* does not survive. After starting at some time and in some measure it is soon destroyed.
>
> Still, as long as there is no offense, even without faith the goal is reached. "Faithfully or Neglectfully, if someone says the Name even once, the goal is gained."[4] "Just hearing the stories (and names) of Hari from the lips of the saintly is ambrosia for the ears. Relishing that continually one develops faith, love and *bhakti* one after the other."[5] Here, first (even before the appearance of faith) there is "ambrosia for the ears" or the taking of pleasure (*ruci*) in the Name. Only after that is there faith. Here, too, as long as there is no offense, even without faith the five forms of *bhakti* headed by *kīrtana* of the Holy Name are said to have an amazing, difficult-to-comprehend power. The example in the *Bhāgavata* on this subject is Ajāmila. Ajāmila gained liberation without faith at the time of his death by means of the semblance or *ābhāsa* of the Holy Name and later he went to Vaikuṇṭha.[6] In this example is revealed the excellence of the giver of such results even for a semblance of *bhakti* (*bhaktyābhāsa*) performed even without faith, as long as there is no offense.
>
> Faith is a kind of certainty about the import of scripture. In other words, becoming certain of and keeping in one's heart all of the ways of attaining Kṛṣṇa that are described in the scriptures is called certainty of the import of scripture, and faith is a form of that. Faith's true nature is trust in the forms of *bhakti* described in scripture. It is not a kind of action. It is not included as an independent form of practice along with other religious practices like hearing, repeating and so forth.

---

[3] *Krama-sandarbha* on Bhāg. 11.20.27.
[4] *Skandha Purāṇa, Prabhāsakhaṇḍa* ?
[5] Bhāg., 3.25.25.
[6] Bhāg., 6.2.49.

Bhakti is not dependent on any rules in order to produce its results, like fire is not dependent on rules in order to burn. Hearing about the Lord, *kīrtana* of His Names and so forth, and the other practices have a natural power like fire does. If so, then how can hearing, *kīrtana* and so forth be dependent on faith? Therefore, even without faith various dullards (like Ajāmila) are found to have reached perfection. Though the word *helā* in the verse: "With faith or with neglect" (*śraddhayā helayā vā*) may mean offense, if that is unintentional then, wickedness being absent, it is not an obstacle to *bhakti*. But the disrespect of a person who, though actually ignorant, is made haughty by a little bit of knowledge *is* an obstacle to *bhakti*. Take for example the sorry state of Vena who repeated the Holy Name with envy. Sometimes, too, it is found that a thing's power is obstructed like the obstruction of the power of fire in wet wood. Offense is the 'wetness' of a living being's mind and the power of *bhakti*, like fire, is in this case obstructed. In order to overcome that obstruction faith is needed. "A devotee who brings me with faith even a handful of water is dear to me, but someone who brings me many offerings of the finest quality, without faith, is not a source of joy for me."[7]

Here the word *śraddhā-bhakti* means respect (*ādara*). Where there is disrespect the Lord is not pleased. A characteristic of offense is disrespect for the Lord. By practicing the various forms of *bhakti* with faith or respect, offense is destroyed and the subtle inclination (*vāsanā*) to serve the Lord with the purpose of making him happy appears. The name of that subtle inclination is love of the Lord. Therefore, the conclusion is that faith is not a form of *bhakti*. But, just as in the realm of rituals there is dependence on the ritualist's wealth, ability and knowledge, so too in this case a candidate for unmixed *bhakti* depends on faith as a qualification. Therefore, in the *Bhāgavata* verse (11.20.8) it is said: "One who somehow has developed faith in stories about me[, neither indifferent nor overly attached, to such a person the yoga of *bhakti* brings success]."[8]

[7] Bhāg., 11.27.17-18.

[8] Jīva, *Krama-sandarbha*, 11.20.27: अतएव यद्यपि ज्ञानकर्मयोरपि श्रद्धापेक्षास्त्येव तां विना बहि-रन्तःसम्यक्प्रवृत्तानुपपत्तेस्तथाप्यत्र श्रद्धामात्रस्य कारणत्वेन विशेषतस्तदङ्गीकारः। अत्रापि च तदपेक्षा

Therefore, Śrī Rūpa in his *Upadeśāmṛta*, in the verse beginning "It may be that the sugar of Kṛṣṇa's Names and sports ... " (*syāt kṛṣṇa-nāma-caritādi-sitāpi ...*), does not merely say, "but every day indeed that [the sugar of Kṛṣṇa's Names, etc.] is still to be taken" *anudinaṃ khalu saiva juṣṭā*. Instead he says, "but every day indeed that is still to be taken *with respect* (*ādarāt*)."[9] This respect or faith is the key to the entire universe of worship. This is so, because aside from offense to the Holy Name, that is, aside from the Holy Name's own displeasure, nothing can prevent the all-powerful *kīrtana* of the Holy Name from producing its results. The destroyer of offense to the Holy Name is faith or respect.

Now the question is: How does that faith arise in the mind of a living being? In the "When, by some chance" (*yadṛcchayā*) verse of the *Bhāgavata Purāṇa* (Bhāg., 11.20.8) an answer is found. Faith appears as a

---

पूर्ववत् सम्यक्प्रवृत्त्यर्थैव; तां विनानन्यताख्या भक्तिस्तथा न प्रवर्तते; कदाचित्किञ्चित्प्रवृत्ता च नश्यतीति। ... भक्तिमात्रं (अपराधरहितो भक्याभासः) तु तां (श्रद्धां) विना सिध्यति; (स्कन्धे प्रभासखण्ढे) सकृदपि परिगीतं श्रद्धया हेलया वा इत्यादौ। (भाग्. ३.२५.२५) सतां प्रसङ्गादित्यादौ च, तत् (श्रद्धायाः) पूर्वतोऽपि तस्याः (अपराधरहिताया भक्त्याभासरूपायाः) फलदातृत्वश्रवणात्, (भाग्., ६.२.४९) म्रियमाणो हरेर्नाम इत्यादौ तया फलदातृत्वसौष्ठवश्रवणाच्च। सा च श्रद्धा शास्त्राभिधेयावधारणस्यैवाङ्गम् तद्विश्वासरूपत्वात्; ततो नानुष्ठानाङ्गत्वे प्रविशति। भक्तिश्च फलोत्पादने विधिसापेक्षापि न स्यात्, दाहादिकर्मणि वह्न्यादिवत्, भगवच्छ्रवणकीर्तनादीनां स्वरूपस्थतादृशशक्तित्वात्। ततस्तस्याः श्रद्धाद्यपेक्षा कुतः स्यात्? अतः श्रद्धां विना क्वचिन्मूढादावपि सिद्धिर्दृश्यते। श्रद्धया हेलया वा इत्यादौ हेला त्वपराधरूपाप्यबुद्धिकृता चेद्दौरात्म्याभावे न भक्तिर्बाध्यते इत्युक्तमेव। ज्ञानलवदुर्विदग्धादौ तु तद्वैपरीत्येन बाध्यते, यथा मत्सरेण नामादिकं गृह्णति वेणो। क्वचिद्वस्तुशक्तिरपि बाधिता दृश्यते, आर्द्रेन्धनादौ वह्निशक्तिरिव। (भाग्., ११.२७.१७-१८) श्रद्धयोपहृतं प्रेष्ठं भक्तेन मम वार्यपि इत्यत्र भूर्यप्यभक्तोपहृतं न मे तोषाय कल्पते इत्यत्र च श्रद्धाभक्तिशब्दाभ्यामादर एवोच्यते; स तु भगवत्तोषलक्षणफलविशेषस्योत्पत्तावनादरलक्षणतद्विघातकापराधस्य निरसनपरः।

तस्माच्छ्रद्धा न भक्त्यङ्गम्, किन्तु कर्मण्यर्थिसमर्थविद्वतावदनन्यताख्यायां भक्तावधिकारिविशेषणमेवेत्यत एव तद्विशेषेणत्वेनैवोक्तम् (८) यदृच्छया मत्कथादौ जातश्रद्धः इति जातश्रद्धः मत्कथासु इति च।

[9] Rūpa, *Upadeśāmṛta*, 7:

> स्यात्कृष्णनामचरितादिसिताप्यविद्या-
> पित्तोपतप्तरसनस्य न रोचिका नु।
> किन्त्वादरादनुदिनं खलु सैव जुष्टा
> स्वाद्वी क्रमाद्भवति तद्गदमूलहन्त्री॥

It may be that the sugar of Kṛṣṇa's Names and games are not pleasing to a tongue fevered by the bile of ignorance. But, if it is tasted every day with respect, gradually that destroyer of the root of the disease [of ignorance] becomes again sweet.

result of the good fortune born of the completely unexpected and unpredictable association with some great one and the great one's bestowing of grace. This may happen in this life or in some previous one.

Moreover, in *Krama-sandarbha* on the *Bhāgavata* verse: "Just hearing the stories (and names) of Hari from the lips of the saintly ... faith, attraction and love will develop in that order." (*satāṃ prasaṅgān mama ... śraddhā ratir bhaktir anukramiṣyati*)[10] Śrī Jīva says: "by hearing about his childhood adventures such as his saving the fallen, killing of the demons Pūtanā and others, at first one's faith or trust arises. After that, gradually one arrives at love." Here the word "acts" (*carita*) is implied because of the word "stories" (*kathā*) found in the source verse. In stories is included names, forms, qualities, and acts. The Name is by its very nature the seed, "the origin of all *bhakti*."[11] From that seed first arises faith which is *bhakti*'s budding sprout. In addition, in the Age of Kali the Name has been mixed with Gaura's compassion: "Victory to the shouts of the syllables 'Hare Kṛṣṇa,' bursting from the lips of Śrī Caitanya, as they flood the world with love." This is Śrī Rūpa's blessing on the world. It cannot become otherwise or be lost, because the names 'Hare Kṛṣṇa' that Śrī Caitanya spoke with his own mouth even today are spread through the atmosphere. Anyone, even in the absence of the saintly as defined by scripture, who performs *kīrtana* of the Name on his own or who reads the Purāṇa of the Name, *Bhāgavata*, will develop faith.

Laghu: Everywhere in scripture one finds it said that after first developing faith one should then listen. Now the question is to what sort of speaker should one listen?

Goswami: The characteristics of the listening teacher (*śravaṇa-guru*) are described in the section on the listening teacher in Jīva's *Bhakti-sandarbha* in this way: "he who has experience in scripture and in the Lord."[12] Moreover, in instructing a reciter of the *Bhāgavata* the characteristics of the listening teacher are revealed:

> One who has found refuge with someone dear to Hari should recite for those who are faithful; without desiring anything from that, being himself satisfied in himself, he becomes successful.[13]

---

[10] Bhāg. 3.25.25. See above.
[11] Cc, 3.20.13.
[12] Bs., 202: शाब्दे परे च निष्णात:
[13] Bhāg., 4.12.50:

The meaning of this verse according to Viśvanātha Cakravartin is this: "Finding refuge with a person dear to Hari, one should recite stories of Hari for faithful listeners and should not accept any kind of payment. The reason for not accepting gifts is that his highest reward is in being filled with joy, thinking: "my reward is that the devotees are mercifully listening to the stories of Hari that I am reciting." Such a speaker achieves success."[14] He is worthy of being a genuine listening teacher.

A faithful believer in scripture therefore desires to listen to a great one who has those kinds of characteristics. But how will a beginning or neophyte practitioner recognize such a great one? Recognition is, after all, a characteristic ability of an intermediate devotee. In addition, that sort of saintly person is not found everywhere because an unerring, great-souled one, though such persons do exist, is very rarely found.

Again in the *Bhakti-sandarbha* it is said that a speaker is either attached or free from attachment. Someone who is given to longing and lust is an attached speaker. His words will not touch the heart. Lacking in good behavior, this sort of person's instruction is rather a cause of harm to people.[15] Then what is the way out? The way out Śrī Jīva describes in another section of the *Bhakti-sandarbha*:

> If one is not fortunate enough to hear stories directly from a great-souled one, then one should narrate them oneself separately. This is because in the Age of Kali reciting the Name and the book of the Name, the *Bhāgavata Purāṇa*, is the main practice. For this reason in [Śrīdhara's] commentary on the *Bhāgavata* verse beginning "Those creations of speech destroy the sins of the people ... " (*tadvāgvisargo*)[16] it is said: if a qualified speaker is available one should listen to the Name and the book of the Name, the *Bhāgavata*; if a hearer is available one should recite them. But if neither are available one should sit alone and recite them.[17]

श्रावयेच्छ्रद्दधानां तीर्थपादप्रियाश्रयः।
नेच्छंस्तत्रात्मनात्मानं सन्तुष्ट इति सिध्यति॥

[14]Viśvanātha's comm. on Bhāg., 4.12.50: नेच्छंस्तद्वेतनं किमपि द्रव्यं न प्रतिगृह्णन्। तत्र हेतुरात्मानं प्रति आत्मनैव सन्तुष्टः, तत्र श्रावणे मत्कथ्यमानां कृष्णकथां भक्तः श्रद्धया शृणोतीत्येतदेव मम वेतनमिति मन्यमान इति सिद्धिं प्राप्नोति।

[15]अपरीक्ष्योपदिष्टं यल्लोकनाशाय तद्भवेत्

[16]Bhāg. 1.5.11.

[17]Jīva, Bs., 261: साक्षादेव महत्कृतस्य कीर्तनस्य श्रवणभाग्यं न सम्पद्यते तदैव स्वयं पृथक्कीर्तनीय-

A person wishing to perform worship should consider one more thing on this subject. "The person to whom I listen should be of the same type of attraction [to Kṛṣṇa] as I am, affectionate by nature, and more advanced than I am."[18] Therefore, it is clear; one cannot just study here or there without any consideration. Some discrimination is necessary.

Laghu: In his *Upadeśāmṛta* Śrī Rūpa said: "The Holy Name does not depend on rules of initiation or any preparatory rites." Therefore if we do not receive initiation into the eighteen syllable mantra[19] can our worship still succeed?

Goswami: Listen to the answer of your question:

> A person who, like a cow or an ass, is always intoxicated by enjoyment of sensual objects and who makes no inquiry, even in dream, into the Lord, into *bhakti*, and into the teacher (*guru*), can, if his mind is without offense, be saved even without a teacher just as Ajāmila was. But [consider] a person with knowledge who knows that Śrī Hari is to be worshipped, that the process of worship brings one to him (Hari), that the teacher is the instructor on this subject, and that many previous great persons have attained Hari on the path of *bhakti* as taught by their teachers. In spite of knowing this, however, that person on the basis of scriptural statements like, "this mantra consisting of the Names of Kṛṣṇa by mere contact with the tongue gives results," and by noting the example of Ajāmila, may think: "What is the need for the hassle of finding a teacher? By simply repeating the Names I will attain the Lord." If so then he becomes guilty of the great offense of disrespecting the teacher and as a result will *not* attain his Lord. Nevertheless, in his current life or in another life, whenever his great offense is diminished, he will find shelter with a teacher and attain to the Lord.[20]

मिति तत्प्राधान्यात्। अत एवोक्तं (भाग्. १.५.११) तद्वाग्विसर्गो जनताघविप्लव इत्यादौ टीकाकृद्भिर्यद्यानि नामानि साधवः महान्तः वक्तरि सति शृण्वन्ति, श्रोतरि सति गृणन्ति, अन्यदा तु स्वयमेव गायन्ति कीर्तयन्ति।

[18] Brs., 1.2.91: स्वजातीयाशये स्निग्धे साधौ स्वतो वरे

[19] The Gopāla-mantra.

[20] Viśvanātha Cakravartin, comm. on Bhāg. 6.2.9-10: ये गोगर्दभादय इव विषयेष्वेवेन्द्रियाणि सदा चारयन्ति, को भगवान् का भक्तिः को गुरुरिति स्वप्नेऽपि न जानन्ति तेषामेव नामाभासादिरीत्या गृहीतहरिनाम्नामजामिलादीनामिव निरपराधानां गुरुं विनापि भवत्येवोद्धारः। हरिर्भजनीय

Laghu: Okay, I understand that taking an initiation-teacher (*dīkṣā-guru*) is necessary, but what kind of person should one have as an initiating teacher?

Goswami: The *Caitanya-caritāmṛta* says: "One who knows the truth about Kṛṣṇa is the teacher."[21] This is the chief definition of the teacher; the rest of the characteristics are secondary. Therefore, the suitability of the teacher is ascertained here through mentioning this one characteristic. If a person who knows the truths about Kṛṣṇa is expert in the conclusions of scripture then that is golden. The teacher's duty is to resolve the questions of the disciple, make his mind firm in the worship, and lead him to the feet of Kṛṣṇa. Therefore, in the *Bhāgavata* the teacher is characterized as "expert in the scriptures and experienced in the highest Brahman, Śrī Kṛṣṇa."[22]

Laghu: I understand, but practically speaking what happens is in most cases exactly the opposite. What can be done?

Goswami: In all circumstances there is a way; the last resort is the most compassionate Holy Name. A person who has not found a teacher who has the characteristics given in scripture can face many bad ends. Such a person has at the very start rejected scripture and made a mistake; this is beyond the pale of all consideration. How can his problem be resolved? He has fallen between two dangers. The unqualified teacher is at some point capable of saying something incorrect, the following of which would bring death and the not following of which would also bring death. Even in this kind of difficulty one cannot reject or disregard the teacher as long as no contempt for or dislike of Viṣṇu or Vaiṣṇavas is evident in him. As long as that is not the case, one has to pay honor to that sort of teacher from afar. Keeping him pleased as far as possible by service from afar and, with faith and respect relying completely on the Holy Name, a practitioner can still succeed in everything.[23]

एव, भजनं तत्प्रापकमेव, तदुपदेष्टा गुरुरेव, गुरूपदिष्टया भक्त्या एव पूर्वे हरिं प्रापुरिति विवेकवि-शेषवत्त्वेऽपि

> नो दीक्षां न च सत्क्रियां न च पुरश्चर्यां मनागीक्षते।
> मन्त्रोऽयं रसनास्पृगेव फलति श्रीकृष्णनामात्मकः॥ इति

प्रमाणदृष्ट्या अजामिलादिदृष्टान्तेन च किं मे गुरुकरणश्रमेण नामकीर्तनादिभिरेव मे भगवत्प्राप्तिर्भाविनी-ति मन्यमानस्तु गुर्ववज्ञालक्षणमहापराधादेव भगवन्तं न प्राप्नोति; किन्तु तस्मिन्नेव जन्मनि जन्मान्तरे वा तदपराधक्षये सति श्रीगुरुचरणाश्रित एव प्राप्नोतीति।

[21] Cc., 2.8.100: *yei kṛṣṇatattvavettā sei guru haya*

[22] Bhāg., 11.3.21.

[23] Jīva Gosvāmin, *Bhakti-sandarbha*, para 237: यः प्रथमं शाब्दे परे च निष्णातमित्याद्युक्तलक्षणं

In that case the teacher remains secondary — in terms of forms of practice he has no influence. There, by the single-form practice of the Holy Name success is achieved.

Therefore beware! Although there is no positive worth in such a teacher — that is, he is not able to drag his students to the feet of Hari — there *is* a thoroughly negative side to such a teacher. By disrespecting him one can commit an offense to the Holy Name, that of disrespecting the teacher. Then even the practitioner's last resort, the Holy Name himself, will not work.

गुरुं नाश्रितवान्, तादृशगुरोश्च मत्सरादितो महाभागवतसत्कारादावनुमतिं न लभते, स प्रथमत एव त्यक्तशास्त्रो न विचार्यते। उभयसङ्कटपातो हि तस्मिन् भवत्येव। एवमादिकाभिप्रायेणैव

> यो वक्ति न्यायरहितमन्यायेन शृणोति यः।
> तावुभौ नरकं घोरं व्रजतः कालमक्षयम्।

इतिनारदपञ्चरात्रे। अतएव दूरत एवाराध्यस्तादृशो गुरुः। वैष्णवविद्वेषी चेत् परित्याज्य एव।

> गुरोरप्यवलिप्तस्य कार्याकार्यमजानतः।
> उत्पथप्रतिपन्नस्य परित्यागो विधीयते॥

इति स्मरणात्

Chapter 6

Divine Love: Easy or Hard to Obtain

Laghu: In our discussions so far it seems that divine love (*prema*) is easy to achieve. But, in the *Bhakti-rasāmṛta-sindhu*[1] love for Hari is said to be very difficult to achieve and is dependent on association with the saintly. Is this not a contradiction?

Goswami: No, there is no contradition. Your understanding is mistaken. If you reflect on Śrī Jīva's commentary the import of that verse can be understood. For instance, (Śrī Rūpa says):

> Love for Hari is very difficult to achieve in two ways. First, even if one engages in many practices for a long time in an 'unskillful' way, it will not be attained. Second, even if that practice is done in a skillful, expert way Hari does not quickly bestow it.[2]

---

[1] Brs., 1.1.35.

[2] Brs, 1.1.35:

साधनौघैरनासङ्गैरलभ्या सुचिरादपि।
हरिना चाश्वदेयेति द्विधा सा स्यात्सुदुर्लभा॥

A lot hinges on the interpretation of this word *anāsaṅga* which is based on *āsaṅga*, which usually means "attachment, devotedness." As an adjective it means "uninterrupted." *Anāsaṅga* would thus have the opposite of those meanings. The literal meaning here would be "by lots of interrupted or intermittant practices it is not obtained even after a

And as evidence he [Rūpa] quotes a verse from the Tantras:

> By the power of knowledge liberation is easily attained, and as a result of the merit of sacrificial rites and such, worldly enjoyment is easily gained, but even by a thousand practices, *bhakti* for Hari is very difficult to attain.[3]

6.1 Love Not Attained by Many Practices

Śrī Jīva comments[4] that at first there is deliberation on the means of attaining enjoyment and liberation as occasioned by the opinion of the Tantra (1.1.36). There, 'performance with *āsaṅga*' is to be added in the matter of knowledge and the merit from sacrificial rites and so forth, because, without *āsaṅga* the cultivation of knowledge and sacrificial rites cannot bring enjoyment and liberation. Forget about their being easy to attain. Here in qualifying the performance of knowledge and rites with the word *āsaṅga*, *āsaṅga* means "being completely intent on that alone" (*tad-eka-niṣṭhatva-mātra*) or being focused only on knowledge and rites; this is the meaning it has. In that case, however, one cannot say that liberation or enjoyment are easy to attain by means of knowledge and rites. In a verse from the *Bhagavad-gītā* (12.5) is it said that those who want to achieve Brahman by means of knowledge face great difficulties in achieving that. And again in the *Bhāgavata* (10.23.9) it is said that those who, out of a desire for the insignificant results of going to heaven and such, are engaged in difficult sacrificial rites are fools who think only they are learned. Therefore, striving for enjoyment and liberation is required to be striving with *āsaṅga* or skillfulness. And this skillfulness consists of joining *bhakti-yoga* with all those practices, because if one does

long while." Or, "by lots of practices lacking in attachment [commitment ?] it is not obtained even after a long while." The translation of *anāsaṅga* as "unskillful" is justifiable on the basis of Jīva's following commentary. The "it" here refers to *bhakti* which Manindra Babu takes as *prema-bhakti* or love. [Trans.]

[3]Brs, 1.1.36:

> ज्ञानतः सुलभा मुक्तिर्भुक्तिर्यज्ञादिपुण्यतः ।
> सेयं साधनसाहस्रैर्हरिभक्तिः सुदुर्लभा ॥

[4]This section and the following one are gists of Śrī Jīva's commentary on Rūpa's discussion of the question of the difficulty of obtaining love for Hari. This section focuses on the verse from the Tantra and the following returns to Rūpa's verse. [Trans.]

not mix in *bhakti*, knowledge and rites are unable to produce any results. Evidence for this is found in the *Bhāgavata* (10.14.5): "In times gone by, many yogīs, after not achieving their goal by the practices of yoga and knowledge, reached the highest goal by worshipping you in the yoga of *bhakti*." And again in the *Bhāgavata* (10.81.19): "Worship of the feet of Śrī Kṛṣṇa is the root cause for the acquisition of all the opulence in heaven, on earth, and in the nether worlds, of all types of success, and even of liberation itself."

In the second half of the verse from the Tantras, *bhakti* for Hari means love (*preman*) for Hari as in the *Bhāgavata* verse (11.3.31): "by *bhakti* [as practice] *bhakti* [as love] is produced."[5] Following this verse from the *Bhāgavata* the word practice (*sādhana*) here means practice connected with Hari, because without connection with Hari practice is not able to produce feeling for Hari. If one takes the word "practice" in the verse to mean worship (*bhajana*, i.e. some form of worship like chanting the Holy Names unmixed with the cultivation of knowledge and rites), then the "being completely intent on that alone" (*āsaṅga*) of the previous verse is arrived at. By this, the meaning of "practice" in the second half of the verse points at pure *bhakti* practices such as chanting the Holy Names. However, with this again is joined the word "thousands," and with that the hope of obtaining love for Kṛṣṇa becomes almost zilch. On top of that, seeing that the prefix "very" (*su*) is added to "difficult to attain" (*durlabha*), out of fear of certain failure no one will enter onto the path of love. Who would labor after something that is beyond reach? But that is not really the conclusion of scripture. In many places in the *Bhāgavata* love is said again and again to be easy to attain. Take, for instance, the *Bhāgavata* verse (2.8.3): "For one who regularly listens with faith to the auspicious stories of Hari or who repeats them, the Lord himself quickly appears in that devotee's heart." And again, in the words of Śrī Nārada (1.5.26): "In that place the sages each day used to sing about the qualities and sports of Hari. By their grace I used to listen to that. In this way, by listening every day with faith my love arose for Hari who is Uttamaḥśloka ([Praised by the] Highest Verses)."

Therefore, it is apparent that taking the word "practice" to mean "pure *bhakti*," as we did above, brings the meaning of the verse into conflict with the conclusions of the *Bhāgavata*. Thus, rejecting that previous meaning we have to search for the correct meaning of the word "practice." For instance, in a verse in the *Bhāgavata* the Lord says: "By the

---

[5] भक्त्या सञ्जातया भक्त्या

practice of yoga I am not attained."[6] Here the word "practice" means a method such as rites and so forth performed for the attainment of Hari. For that reason the word "practice" (*sādhana*) and not "worship" (*bhajana*) is used here. Being devoted to practice now means performing with skillfulness practices like rites and so forth for the purpose of attaining Hari. It is thus said that *bhakti* for Hari is very difficult to achieve by thousands and thousands of even skillfully performed practices like rites and yoga and so forth. This is done in order to promote the idea that living beings should undertake worship in the form of chanting of the Holy Names and so forth instead [of rites, yoga, knowledge, and so forth]. It is said so that the living being not head in the direction of an impossibility but rather take the easy path to love, the path of *bhakti* in the form of chanting of the Holy Names.

6.2 Love Not Easily Given by Hari

Even if practice is expertly performed, Hari does not easily bestow love for himself.[7] The evidence for this is in the Fifth Canto of the *Bhāgavata* (5.6.18): "O king, Lord Mukunda was the protector of you Yadus, your guru, your object of honor, your friend, and the controller of your family. From time to time he even acted as a messenger for you like one of your servants. The kind of gracefulness that Mukunda showed in his dealings with you he never bestows on those who worship him, though he grants them liberation."[8]

In the commentary is it said that the word *karhicit* in the verse gives the meaning that he does not "at some time" give *bhakti*. "At some time" means in some conditions of the mind of the practitioner. What are those conditions? The conditions are when the mind contains desires for other things and offenses to the Holy Name. If the verse meant "never at all" then the words *karhicid api* would have been used. Since that is not

---

[6]Bhāg. 11.14.20: न साधयति मां योग:

[7] Brs 1.1.35, second half. See above.

[8]Bhāg., 5.6.18:

राजन् पतिर्गुरुरलं भवतां यदूनां
दैवं प्रियः कुलपतिः क्क च किङ्करो वः।
अस्त्वेवमङ्ग भगवान् भजतां मुकुन्दो
मुक्तिं ददाति कर्हिचित्स्म न भक्तियोगम्॥

the wording in the verse its meaning is that the most compassionate Śrī Kṛṣṇa does not give love to a person who has the faults of offense to the Holy Name and desire for other things. But when those faults have been eliminated and a deep attachment to chanting the Holy Names and so forth is born, then he gives it.

There is also a special consideration here. The most compassionate, foremost of enjoyers of *rasa*, Śrī Kṛṣṇa has this time come, uniting his body with his beloved, the highest of his devotees, out of an irrepressible desire to give the gift of divine love on a large scale. As a result, that love is bestowed on anyone, whether one asks for it or not. Saying "Hari Hari," in whatever direction he casts his loving glance he destroys all impurities and floods it with divine love — Śāntipura is submerged and flooded by that river. Even after that flood of love during his time has gone, everything still remains. Only one little rule has been added, that in his time did not exist: "If one chants the Holy Names without offense one gets the treasure of love."[9] In the meantime, the question of his not giving it has become immaterial. Now the question is only in what way and how soon will we accept it. The giving hand is extended out. It only depends on our shedding our offense. As soon as we are able to put aside the impurities of our minds, that is, our offenses and so forth, the substance of love will come into our possession. Where offense is great more intense effort is needed. An unceasing burnishing is needed, a polishing by the non-material substance, the Holy Names, of the mind smeared with the grime of material filth. The *Padma Purāṇa* says: "And those [Names] applied unceasingly are effective."[10] In the case of offense the delay depends on when that is eliminated. In a case of freedom from offense, Śrī Rūpa has spoken of the hard-to-understand, amazing potency of the best five forms of *bhakti*, headed by chanting the Holy Names, and of the extreme ease with which love is attain by means of them.[11]

To summarize Śrī Jīva's long commentary:

1. The meaning of the word *āsaṅga* is "skillfulness." This skillfulness in the practices of performing rites, yoga and so forth is mixing them with *bhakti*. If one performs those practices with such skillfulness, then enjoyment and liberation are easy to attain.

---

[9]Cc. 3. 4.71.

[10]*Padma Purāṇa*, Sarga, 48.54: अविश्रान्तप्रयुक्तानि तान्येव अर्थकराणि च

[11]Brs. 1.2.238: दुरुहाद्भुतवीर्येऽस्मिन् ...

2. But by thousands and thousands of such practices love for Kṛṣṇa is very difficult to attain. The point of that statement is to encourage the performance of pure *bhakti* practices such as *kīrtana* of the Holy Names and so forth.

3. By the grace of Śrī Gaurahari, in this present Age of Kali not only is love for Kṛṣṇa easy to attain, but the best of all forms of love, Rādhā's type of love, is easy to attain. "If one chants the Holy Names without offense, one gets the treasure of love."[12]

[12] Cc., Antya, 4.66: *niraparādha nām haite hoy premadhan*

Chapter 7

Saṅkīrtana in Multi-formed Practice

Laghu: Okay, I understand practice and achievement through one form. Now tell me about practicing using many forms.

Goswami: Look, whether in one form or in many the seed is one and it, as the whole, causes other forms, its limbs, to appear — that is, the chanting of the Holy Names. Apart from that there is nothing else that can clean the mirror of the mind — "the Names alone take away sin" (*nāmānyeva harantyagham*) — the use of the word *eva* (alone) emphasizes that here.

Just as a chaste wife takes shelter wholeheartedly in her husband, for the purpose of his happiness serves him devotedly, and by that becomes complete in herself, not wishing for anything for herself, so it is with a wise practitioner who, knowing that the Name is the best of all, chooses in his heart with great respect the Name as the master of his life and serves him. In that he becomes full and complete. There is no reason for him to even glance in the direction of any other form of *bhakti*. Similarly, though there is no need for the husband to be pleased with the devoted service of his wife, he sometimes gives her a gift and since it is a gift from her husband the wife accepts it with great respect.[1] In the same way the Name sometimes causes some other form of *bhakti*, like remembering

[1]This simile pushes the good, chaste wife and husband-as-god ideal a bit far even for Indian society. [Trans.]

(*smaraṇa*) and so forth, to appear in the mind of his devoted servant. Since it is the gift of the Holy Name the practitioner accepts it with great respect. Thus, the forms of *bhakti* one undertakes can become two, three, or even more. In this way even remembering, which is the main form of passion-pursuing (*rāgānugā*) *bhakti*, comes to be adopted as a form of practice. Now the question arises: What condition does the mind have to be in in order for the Name to bestow remembering? Śrī Jīva Gosvāmin says: "If the mind is pure (*śuddha*), then without giving up chanting of the Names one may perform remembering."[2]

Notice that here the word *śuddha* has been used, not *viśuddha* (completely pure). From that one can understand that the intent here is not to say that only when the mind is completely pure or completely free from offense is one qualified to practice remembering. In that condition, the condition of being completely cleansed of stains, that is, on the level of having successfully reached the goal, the question of forms of practice or cultivation is irrelevant. Therefore, Śrī Jīva is talking about only partial purity of the mind here — when the mind is partially purified one may practice remembering.

The *Bhāgavata* has a verse on this topic (11.14.26):

> To the degree that the mind is cleansed by hearing of and repeating my auspicious deeds one becomes able to see my forms, qualities and sports, like [someone with] eyes dabbed with medicinal ointment."[3]

In what state of purity does this capacity become complete? That discussion is found in Viśvanātha Cakravartin's *Mādhurya-kādambinī* (Cloud-bank of Sweetness), in the Fourth Downpour (Chapter Four): "after the stage of cessation of harmful habits, on the stage of steadiness (*niṣṭhā*)[4]

---

[2]Śrī Jīva in the *Krama-sandarbha* on Bhāg. 7.5.25: शुद्धान्तःकरणश्चेन्नामकीर्तनापरित्यागेन स्मरणं कुर्यात्।

[3]Bhāg. 11.14.26:

> यथा यथात्मा परिमृज्यतेऽसौ
> मत्पुण्यगाथाश्रवणाभिधानैः।
> तथा तथा पश्यति वस्तुसूक्ष्मं
> चक्षुर्यथैवाञ्जनसम्प्रयुक्तम्॥

[4]Viśvanātha Cakravartin, Mk., 4: अनर्थनिवृत्त्यनन्तरं तेषां तदीयानां प्रायत्वान्नैश्चल्यं सम्पद्यते। The first stage of *bhakti* is faith (*śraddhā*). This is the 'gate pass' into the kingdom of

when the five obstacles (sleep, distraction, lack of determination, impurity of mind, and the taste for flavors of the sense objects)[5] are nearly overcome then *bhakti* becomes unshakable.

When in that way unwavering *bhakti* arises, the mind is not conquered by lust, anger and so forth which are produced by the material qualities of dimness (*rajas*) and darkness (*tamas*). Instead, the mind only becomes attached to the Lord, who is pure goodness embodied, and becomes peaceful.[6]

Therefore, we see that the mind is able to enter steadily into the sports, qualities, forms and names of the Lord at the stage of steadiness. Before that, when still at the stage of cessation of harmful habits, the harmful tendencies are at least two thirds destroyed — attachment to the sense objects is weaker and attachment to Kṛṣṇa is stronger — the scales are leaning in Kṛṣṇa's direction. Even at that stage remembering does not occur; one can only attempt to practice remembering. Therefore Kṛṣṇa says:

> Hey Dhanañjaya! If you are not able to fix your mind steadily on me, try by the yoga of repetitive discipline to attain me. [7]

Viśvanātha's comment on this verse is: "When the mind has gone somewhere else, repeatedly pull it back from there and place it on my form. That is repetitive discipline (*abhyāsa*), that is *yoga*. By this yoga of repetitive discipline turn the current of the river-like mind that flows to

---

bhakti. "A person with faith is qualified for *bhakti*" (Cc., 2.22.38). The state of mind of a practitioner on this stage is: "by faith one means confidence, the strong certainty that if one performs *bhakti* for Kṛṣṇa all rites and acts are thereby accomplished" (Cc., 2.22.27). The second stage is association with saintly persons (*sādhu-saṅga*). At this stage one offers oneself to Kṛṣṇa (Cc., 2.22.53). The third stage, called engagement in worship (*bhajana-kriyā*), is represented by the sixty-four forms of practice beginning with taking shelter at the feet of a teacher. The fourth stage is cessation of harmful habits (*anartha-nivṛtti*) and the fifth is unwavering steadiness (*niṣṭhā*).

[5] *Laya* — falling asleep during worship or meditation (*bhajana*); *vikṣepa* — the wandering of the mind again and again to the sense objects during worship; *apratipatti* — losing one's desire for it after engaging in worship for a short while; *kaṣāya* — impurity of the mind; and *rasāsvāda* — a liking for the flavors or pleasures of the sense objects.

[6] ibid.

[7] *Bhagavad-gītā* (Bg), 12.9:

अथ चित्तं समाधातुं न शक्नोषि मयि स्थिरम्।
अभ्यासयोगेन ततो मामिच्छाप्तुं धनञ्जय॥

gross material forms and feelings gradually away from them and in the direction of my auspicious, supremely beautiful forms and feelings."[8]

In this way when the mind becomes steady through practicing this yoga of repetition, a practitioner "performs hearing and *kīrtana* in his external, practitioner's body and, visualizing in his mind an accomplished body, serves Kṛṣṇa in Vraja day and night."[9] This is the interstate highway of worship for those who follow in the footsteps of Śrī Gaura. From *saṅkīrtana* of the Holy Names the joy of meditation (i.e., remembering) increases, and that increased joy of meditation increases one's enjoyment of the sweetness of *saṅkīrtana*. We partake of both the joy of *saṅkīrtana* and the joy of meditation.[10] Moment by moment both increase. Neither ever diminishes.

How does continuing practice of *saṅkīrtana* of the Holy Names bring about entry into the divine play? Śrī Gaurahari has given us a peek at that in order to teach us. "Govinda used to sleep at the door of Gambhīrā.[11] In the middle of the night the Master did loud *saṅkīrtana*. Suddenly, the Master heard Kṛṣṇa's flute. Overwhelmed by emotion the Master went there."[12] Not hearing the Master the devotees began to search for him. Finally at the Lion Gate of the Jagannātha Temple they found him lying unconscious in the middle of some Tailaṅga cows, his body folded together in the shape of a turtle. While they performed loud *saṅkīrtana* of the Holy Names the Master became conscious again. Staring at the devotees he began to speak:

> Sitting up, the Master looked about here and there. He said to Svarūpa: "Where have you taken me? Hearing the sound of the flute I went to Vṛndāvana. I saw Vrajendranandana (Son of the Leader of Vraja, ie. Kṛṣṇa) playing his flute in the meadows. By the indication of the flute's sound, Rādhā went to the bower hut. Kṛṣṇa, too, went to the bower for the play of love. I followed after him, a little bit behind. My sense of hearing was stolen away by the sounds of his ornaments. He

---

[8] Viśvanātha's comm on Bg., 12.9: अभ्यासयोगेन अन्यत्रान्यत्र गतमपि मनः पुनः पुनः प्रत्याहृत्य मद्रूप एव स्थापनमभ्यासः स एव योगस्तेन प्राकृतत्वादिति कुत्सितरूपरसादिषु चलन्त्या मनोनद्यास्तेषु चलनं निरुध्यातिसुभद्रेषु मदीयरूपरसादिषु तच्चलनं शनैः शनैः सम्पादय इत्यर्थः।

[9] Cc., Madhya 22.89.

[10] Sanātana, Bb., 2.3.53: श्रीसङ्कीर्तनाद्ध्यानसुखं विवर्धते ध्यानाच्च सङ्कीर्तनमाधुरीसुखम्। And in Sanātana's commentary: वयं तु ध्यानं सङ्कीर्तनञ्च द्वयमेव सेव्यं मन्यामहे।

[11] This is the name of the room that Śrī Caitanya used to sleep in when he lived in Purī.

[12] Cc., Antya 10.79-80.

> enjoyed joking and laughing with the cowherd girls. Hearing his voice and words my ears were thrilled."[13]

This is Śrī Gaurahari's relishing in the identity of a *mañjarī*. See, "the defining characteristic of the successful becomes the practice of the practitioner."[14] Following this logic the practitioner, too, performing *saṅkīrtana* of the Holy Names and remembering Śrī Gaurahari in Gambhīrā, assimilates his feelings with those of Śrī Gaura and is able to go to the bower of Rādhā and Govinda in Vṛndāvana in the form of a *mañjarī*.

Therefore, from the foregoing discussion one learns that one should not start the remembering form of *bhakti* when the mind is in just any condition or by merely memorizing the texts. In order to attain the proper qualification for the practice of remembering one needs a regular practice — and that practice is *saṅkīrtana* of the Holy Names. "Cleansing the mirror of the mind" (*ceto-darpana-mārjanaṃ*) When the proper qualification is achieved, the condition of one's mind appears like this: "if one performs *bhakti* for Kṛṣṇa, all actions are thereby complete — one offers oneself to Kṛṣṇa — the great forest fire of worldly becoming is put out." If a practitioner, finding that his own condition matches the one described above, proceeds in the direction of remembering, then real blessedness can be attained.

Again when, with the attainment of proper qualification, one begins the practice of remembering, *saṅkīrtana* of the Holy Names remains the main form of practice. To exclude that will not work.

A process is given in the *Bhakti-sandarbha* for performing this practice of remembering beginning with the Names and then moving on to the forms, qualities and sports in that order. What is meant by the remembering of the Names is indicated to some degree below.

7.1 Remembering the Holy Names

Śrī Jīva cites a verse from the *Jabāli-saṃhitā* in his *Bhakti-sandarbha*:

---

[13]Cc., 3.17.9-27.

[14]Sanātana, comm. on Bb., 2.6.165. परमात्यां विचित्रमधुरगाथाप्रबन्धेन भगवन्नामसङ्कीर्तनं कार्यमिति तात्पर्यं सिद्धस्य लक्षणं यत्स्यात्साधनं साधकस्य तदिति न्यायात्

> The Name of Hari is by all means to be chanted (*japya*), meditated on, sung and loudly repeated (*kīrtanīya*) without ceasing by one who intensely desires the fullest of joys.[15]

And he adds: "But remembering of the Names depends upon a purified mind."[16]

Śrī Sanātana discusses what this remembering of the Names is in his commentary on *Bṛhad-bhāgavatāmṛta* verse 1.1.9: "Victory, victory again to that embodiment of joy, the Name of Murāri ..." While describing the engagement of all the senses in the Holy Names he says: "the engagement in the Holy Names by the mind means recalling the syllables of the Names."[17] Previously it was said that without giving up *saṅkīrtana* of the Holy Names one may engage in remembering. Therefore, when one does *kīrtana* of the Names that are dear to one, like Kṛṣṇa, Govinda, Rādhā, Gaura, and so forth, the syllables of those names in Sanskrit, or Bengali, or whatever language one pleases, should be remembered. To make visual recalling more easy, it is good to write largely and clearly the syllables of the Names on the walls of one's room or on paper. Just as the Lord manifests his countless forms for the eyes and the ears in accordance with the feelings of his devotees, so too are the syllables of his names able to appear in many forms in Sanskrit, Bengali, and other languages. This remembering of the Names is mentioned in the dialogue between Rāmānanda Rāya and Mahāprabhu in this way:

> The Lord: "What is to be remembered?"
>
> Rāya: "The names of the Enemy of Agha (Kṛṣṇa)."[18]

Laghu: What is the easiest way to enter into the realm of the remembering form of *bhakti*?

Goswami: Remembering is a function of the mind. The mind is as inconstant as the wind. Bringing it under control is a very difficult job.

---

[15] Bs., 273.

> हरेर्नाम परं जप्यं ध्येयं गेयं निरन्तरम्।
> कीर्तनीयञ्च बहुधा निर्वृतिर्बहुधेच्छता॥

[16] ibid. नामस्मरणस्तु शुद्धान्तःकरणतामपेक्षते

[17] Sanātana's comm. on Bb., 1.1.9. तत्रान्तःकरणैस्तस्य ग्रहणं नामाक्षरादिचिन्तनरूपम्

[18] Kavi Karṇapūra, Ccn., Act 7, verse 10. भगवान् — किं स्मरणीयं; रामानन्द — अघारिनाम See also Cc., 2.8.206.

> Kṛṣṇa! The mind is by nature unstable, disturbing, powerful, and strong. Bringing such a thing under control is as difficult as controlling the wind.[19]

The world teacher, Śrī Gaurahari, has revealed a beautiful and clever way for easily catching that slippery mind and engaging it in the names, forms, qualities, and sports of the Lord. He has revealed it through the pen of his close companion Śrī Sanātana Gosvāmin:

> I consider *kīrtana* better than remembrance appearing spontaneously in the unsteady mind. When it (*kīrtana*) appears on the tongue it is also registered in the mind and the hearing. Moreover, it then helps others in addition to oneself.[20]

Sanātana adds in his commentary: "In addition, without *kīrtana* the mind is unable to gain the capacity for remembering, because there is no other way to steady the naturally unsteady mind. In an unsteady mind remembrance cannot take place."[21]

The phrase "also registered in the mind" in this verse is particularly worthy of close attention. By means of *kīrtana* the names, forms, qualities, and sports by themselves become connected with the mind. Those things that run away when one tries to capture them come of their own accord and allow themselves to be held like snakes when they hear the flute of the snake-charmer. What amazing magic this *saṅkīrtana* of the Holy Names is!

Therefore the great teacher of *rasa*, Śrī Rūpa Gosvāmin, has given an instruction that is the essence of all instructions in the summary verse

---

[19] Bg., 6.34.

चञ्चलं हि मनः कृष्ण प्रमाथि बलवद्दृढं।
तस्याहं निग्रहं मन्ये वायोरिव सुदुष्कृतम्॥

[20] Bb., 2.3.148.

मन्यामहे कीर्तनमेव सत्तमं
लोलात्मकैकस्वहृदि स्फुरत्स्मृतेः।
वाचि स्वयुक्ते मनसि श्रुतौ तथा
दीव्यत्परानप्युपकुर्वदात्मवत्॥

[21] Sanātana, comm. on Bb., 2.3.184. अथ च मनसश्च स्वभावापनयनेन वशीकरणानुपपत्तेः स्मरणमपि न सम्यक्सिध्यतीति गूढोऽभिप्रायः

in his discussion of passionate worship: "Practitioners on the Path of Passion! After performing *saṅkīrtana* of the Names and the rest, cultivate remembering in accordance with that."

> Performing *saṅkīrtana* of Kṛṣṇa's names, forms, qualities and sports and then after *saṅkīrtana*, remembering them in accordance with that, with tongue and mind engaged in that way and in that order, one should follow those who truly love him (Kṛṣṇa) and spend one's entire life living in Vraja. This is the essence of my instruction.[22]

Laghu: What are the rules for chanting Kṛṣṇa's Names?

Goswami: That Śrī Gaurahari himself taught the people of Navadvīpa with the rest of the world in mind:

> Feeling an intense thrill the Master gave this instruction:
> "Hear with special care the Great Mantra of Kṛṣṇa's Names:
> *hare kṛṣṇa hare kṛṣṇa*
> *kṛṣṇa kṛṣṇa hare hare;*
> *hare rāma hare rāma*
> *rāma rāma hare hare."*
> The Master said: "This is the Great Mantra.
> Chant (*japa*) this, everyone, with perseverence.
> From this all successes will come to all.
> Every moment say it, in this there is no other rule.
> Five or ten of you gathering, sitting at your doors,
> do *kīrtana* clapping your hands:
> *haraye namaḥ kṛṣṇa yādavāya namaḥ*
> *gopāla govinda rāma śrīmadhusūdana*
> This *kīrtana* I have told to all of you.
> Wives, sons, and fathers gathering together,
> do it in your homes.[23]

---

[22] Rūpa, *Upadeśāmṛta*, 8.

> तन्नामरूपचरितादिसुकीर्तनानु-
> स्मृत्योः क्रमेण रसनामनसी नियोज्य।
> तिष्ठन्व्रजे तदनुरागिजनानुगामी
> कालं नयेदखिलमित्युपदेशसारम्॥

[23] Vṛndāvana Dāsa, *Caitanya-bhāgavata* (Cb)., Madhya 23.75-89.

Putting all this together into one prescription or process, one has in brief this: With the *Hare Kṛṣṇa* Great Chant (*mahāmantra*) one should do counted repetitions (*japa*) and uncounted *kīrtana* or *saṅkīrtana*. On top of that one should do *saṅkīrtana* of one's own preferred or beloved names of Kṛṣṇa. In the Gauḍīya community the preferred names are generally Gaura, Kṛṣṇa, Rādhā, and so forth. By the *saṅkīrtana* of those beloved names *bhakti* becomes ignited.[24] Although all of the forms of the Lord have the same greatness, by *saṅkīrtana* of those names that are specially dear to one one quickly reaches one's goal and attains the joy of divine love (*preman*).[25]

The first teacher of *bhakti*, sage of the gods, Nārada made a request of Kṛṣṇa: "Master! I have now seen for myself that the cowherd women of Vraja are the highest recipients of your grace. Please grant me a wish:

> Royal Swan wandering in the love-lake of the people of Vraja! May I wander like a drunkard through the universe, giving joy to all the worlds, drinking repeatedly and ceaselessly [doing repeated and ceaseless *kīrtana* of] your sweeter-than-sweet, ambrosial Names arising out of that milk-ocean of Gokula and revealing your forms and sports there.[26]

āpane hariṣe prabhu kare upadeśa
kṛṣṇanāma mahāmantra śunaha viśeṣa
hare kṛṣṇa hare kṛṣṇa kṛṣṇa kṛṣṇa hare hare
hare rāma hare rāma rāma rāma hare hare
prabhu bale kahilām ei mahāmantra
ihā japa giyā sabe kariyā nirbandha
ihā haite sarvasiddhi haibe sabāra
sarvakṣaṇa bala ithe vidhi nāhi āra
daśa-pāñca mili nija dvāvete basiyā
kīrtana karaha sabe hāte tāli diyā
haraye namaḥ kṛṣṇa yādavāya namaḥ
gopāla govinda rāma śrīmadhusūdana
kīrtana kahila e tomā sabākāre
strīputra bāpe mili kara giyā ghare

[24] Bb., 2.5.218. प्रेष्ठनामसङ्कीर्तनोज्ज्वलम्

[25] Bb., 2.3.160.

सर्वेषां भगवन्नाम्नां समानो महिमापि चेत्।
तथापि स्वप्रियेणाशु स्वार्थसिद्धिः सुखं भवेत्॥

[26] Bb., 1.7.143.

पायं पायं व्रजजनगणप्रेमवापीमराल

That first teacher Nārada has given us a peek at the worship of practitioners who desire to serve Rādhā in this verse. Now here is our humble request at Śrī Nārada's feet: "Fill us with grace so that we are able to follow the path you have indicated — so that, while singing the names 'Gaura, Kṛṣṇa, Rādhā' with melody, rhythm, and tempo to the accompaniment of hand cymbals and drums we may float in the bliss of divine love." Although all the Names of Gokula have equal sweetness, as one performs worship one's mind tarries over a specific name according to one's mood or feelings. That then is that person's dearest name. Jaya Rādhe!

Laghu: Chanting (*japa*), *kīrtana*, and *saṅkīrtana*; what is the difference between them and which of them is the best?

Goswami: Chanting (*japa*) means repeated pronunciation, according to rules, of the *mantra* (a verbal, formulaic evocation in Sanskrit) of one's desired deity. It is of three types: vocal, whispered or silent (mentally repeated). Among the different types of chanting, vocal chanting or the audibly vocal pronunciation of the Holy Names while they are counted is the best.[27] *Kīrtana* is loud pronunciation and *saṅkīrtana* is *kīrtana* in the form of sweet songs and rhythms — in *saṅkīrtana* there are melody, rhythm, and tempo. In *kīrtana* there isn't.[28] Among the three forms of cultivation of the Holy Name mentioned above, chanting, *kīrtana*, and *saṅkīrtana*, the latter is the best of all.[29] Gaura and Nitai are called the fathers of *saṅkīrtana*, not of chanting (*japa*).[30] *Saṅkīrtana* was initiated and bestowed by them; it is dear to the heart of Śrī Gaurahari. Therefore, he has praised it as the highest of all in his eight verses of instruction: "Highest of glories to the *saṅkīrtana* of Kṛṣṇa" (*paraṃ vijayate śrīkṛṣṇasaṅkīrtanam*).

Laghu: Why are there so many rules, since in scripture it is said that in whatever way one says the Holy Name one can reach the desired

---

श्रीमन्नामामृतमविरतं गोकुलाब्ध्युत्थितं ते।
तत्तद्वेशाचरितनिकरोज्जृम्भितं मिष्टमिष्टं
सर्वाँल्लोकान् जगति रमयन्मत्तचेष्टो भ्रमाणि॥

[27]Jīva Gosvāmin, Ks. on Bhāg., 7.5.25: नामकीर्तनञ्चेदमुच्चैरेव प्रशस्तम्.

[28]Sanātana, comm. on Bb., 2.1.104: सङ्कीर्तनं नाम्नां श्रीकृष्णगोविन्दगोपालेत्यादीनां यत्सम्यङ्म-धुरस्वरगाथया कीर्तनमुच्चैरुच्चारणम्।

[29]Cc., 3.3.75:

japakartā haite uccasaṅkīrtanakārī
śataguṇa adhika se purāṇete dhari

[30]Vṛndāvana Dāsa, Cb., 1.1.1: सङ्कीर्तनैकपितरौ.

goal?

Goswami: Yes, one can reach it; still, look, the sages have created the rules for your benefit. If one breaks those, at the very start one becomes guilty of the offense of disrespecting the teacher. As a result of that even the Holy Name ceases to act. An experienced doctor who understands the nature of a disease in his prescription orders three forms of the medicine, penicillin — a cream, a syrup, and an injection. Now if through your own speculations you use the first two types, but reject the third, the injection-form, which is the most effective of all, then what help are you able to get in that? If a practitioner is to be fully benefitted, doing both counted chanting and *saṅkīrtana* is necessary.

Śrī Gaurahari has himself indicated that one hundred thousand names is the smallest number of names acceptable for the practice of chanting (*japa*):[31] "When invited for a meal the Master said with a smile: 'First you become lords of a hundred thousand.'"[32] If the Master will not come to one's house, then what is the purpose of worshipping? Therefore, the Master fixed the number of names at one hundred thousand.

When the temperature increases, the mercury of a thermometer naturally moves upwards, too. So it is that when a person's enthusiastic effort and eagerness increase, with the weakening and destruction of their offenses as a result of chanting the Holy Names, the number of Holy Names chanted also increases. The goal is to be always doing *kīrtana* of the Holy Names.[33] If one wants to arrive at that goal, one has to approach it through the counted chanting — this is the general rule. This is generally noticed also in the manner of worship followed by great saints who have reached the ultimate goal through practice. *Kīrtanīyaḥ sadā hariḥ*, "Hari is always to be praised." Whether one is a householder or a renunciant, Gaurahari taught that this is the goal for all living beings. That is the natural characteristic of the self. There is no distinction in the characteristics of the self — the self is neither a householder nor a renunciant. The living being's true nature is to be an eternal servant of Kṛṣṇa:

[31] One hundred thousand names equals 64 rounds on a Vaiṣṇava set of beads, which has 108 beads on it. Each bead represents 16 names chanted.

[32] Cb., 3.9.117:

> *bhikṣā nimantraṇe prabhu balen hāsiyā*
> *cala tumi āge lakṣeśvara hao giyā*

[33] *Śikṣāṣṭaka*, 3: कीर्तनीयः सदा हरिः

> I am not a priest, nor a king, nor a tradesman, nor a serf. I am not a student, householder, retiree nor renunciant. I am but the servant of the servant of the servant of the lotus feet of that lover of the cowherd women [Kṛṣṇa], who is an ocean of the most extraordinary of all joys.[34]

Just as chanting is to be done regularly, *saṅkīrtana* should be done regularly as well. Whether in the morning or the evening, one should choose a time that is convenient and every day at that time engage in *saṅkīrtana*. One should perform *saṅkīrtana*, with the intention of being compassionate, for a determined amount of time each day, a half an hour or an hour. Gradually if one can increase that time and fix it at two hours a day it is good. At first it is a matter of disciplined repetition, but later it becomes a deep-seated inclination. One can perform *saṅkīrtana* alone or with others, if one has the association of others with the same kind of attraction.

7.2 The Distinctiveness of *Saṅkīrtana* in Multi-form Practice

Śrī Sanātana Gosvāmin has described in this way the practice to attain the kind of love seen in Vraja in his *Bṛhad-bhāgavatāmṛta*:

> The love as seen in Vraja is attained by *bhakti* in which meditation on and songs about the sports of Vraja predominate and which is made manifest by *saṅkīrtana* of the names of one's dearest one.[35]

---

[34]Śrī Caitanya, as cited in Rūpa's collection, the *Padyāvalī*, 74:

> नाहं विप्रो न च नरपतिर्नापि वैश्यो न शूद्रो
> नो वा वर्णी न च गृहपतिर्नो वनस्थो यतिर्वा।
> किन्तु प्रोद्यन्निखिलपरमानन्दपूर्णामृताब्धे-
> र्गोपीभर्तुः पदकलमयोर्दासदासानुदासः॥

[35]Bb., 2.5.218:

> तद्धि तत्तद्व्रजक्रीडाध्यानगानप्रधानया।
> भक्त्या सम्पद्यते प्रेष्ठनामसङ्कीर्तनोज्ज्वलम्॥

In his commentary on the verse the respected Gosvāmin says:

> The means for attaining that love of Vraja is here being described. By means of that ninefold *bhakti* in which remembering and *saṅkīrtana* of the Gokula (Vraja) sports of the Lover of Rādhā (Kṛṣṇa) dominate, that love is attained.
>
> Here an important distinction is being made. In the statement "made manifest by *saṅkīrtana* of the names of one's dearest one" (*preṣṭhanāmasaṅkīrtanojjvalam*), it is said that the love of Vraja arises from *saṅkīrtana* of the names that are dearest to one. But songs was mentioned before along with remembering (meditation) and certainly *saṅkīrtana* of the names is included in that. Therefore why is *saṅkīrtana* of the names mentioned again? There is a purpose for it and that is to indicate that the *saṅkīrtana* of the names most dear to one is a more essential means. That is, remembering and singing are important, but *saṅkīrtana* of the Holy Names is even more germane. Therefore it has been mentioned again as special.[36]

It is necessary to try and honor what Śrī Sanātana Gosvāmin, who has everyone's well-being at heart, has etched in letters of gold, as it were, in his words above.

In the *Bhāgavata* the object of worship and the manner of worship is described in the "dark color" (*kṛṣṇa-varṇam*) verse.[37] There, the highest limit of the supreme truth, Gaurahari, is ascertained as the object of worship and *saṅkīrtana* of the Holy Names as his primary manner of worship.

In his commentary on this verse, Śrī Jīva says: "The best article to be offered in the worship of Gaurahari, the father of *saṅkīrtana*, is *saṅkīrtana*

---

[36]Sanātana's comm. on Bb., 2.5.218: अधुना साधनमाह — तद्धीति। तासां तासां व्रजक्रीडानां भगवद्गोकुललीलानां ध्यानं चिन्तनं गानं सङ्कीर्तनं ते प्रधाने मुख्ये यस्यास्तया नवप्रकारया प्रेम सम्पद्यते सुसिध्यति। तत्रैव विशेषमेकमाह — प्रेष्ठस्य निजेष्टतमदेवस्य प्रेष्ठानां वा निजप्रियतमानां भगवन्नाम्नां सङ्कीर्तनेन उज्ज्वलं प्रकाशमानं शुद्धं वा। गानेत्युक्त्वा नामसङ्कीर्तने प्राप्तेऽपि निजप्रियतमनामसङ्कीर्तनस्य प्रेमान्तरङ्गतरसाधनत्वेन पुनर्विशेषेण निर्देशः। किंवा तत्सम्पत्तिलक्षणज्ञानाय।

[37]Bhāg., 11.5.32:

> कृष्णवर्णं त्विषाकृष्णं साङ्गोपाङ्गास्त्रपार्षदम्।
> यज्ञैः सङ्कीर्तनप्रायैर्यजन्ति हि सुमेदसः॥

With sacrifices, primarily consisting of *saṅkīrtana*, the wise worship him whose syllables are "kṛṣ-ṇa," whose complexion is not dark (ie., light), and who is surrounded by his major limbs, minor limbs, weapons, and companions.

of the Names of Kṛṣṇa. Among all the various articles for offering like flowers, sandalwood, hearing, praising and so forth, *saṅkīrtana* of the Names should remain the primary one. Then he is pleased. *Saṅkīrtana* is the loud vocalization of Kṛṣṇa's Names, either alone or with other people, performed with melody, rhythm, and tempo and with drums, hand-cymbals, and other instruments. Even among Gaurahari's own close followers, *saṅkīrtana* of the Names was seen as primary. Clearly, it is the best way of creating Gaurahari's affection.[38]

If we today take this clear statement as unclear because we are not paying due attention[39] to the words of the Gosvāmins, then what else can we be called but foolish unfortunates? Therefore the author of the *Caitanya-caritāmṛta* has said:

> The initiator of *saṅkīrtana*
> is Śrī Kṛṣṇa Caitanya.
> Through the rite of *saṅkīrtana*
> one who worships him is
> both fortunate and very smart;
> all the rest is foolish worldliness.
> The rite of Kṛṣṇa's Name
> is the essence of all rites.[40]

Although sometimes and in some places *saṅkīrtana* of the Holy Names is seen even among worldly fools, they do not see *saṅkīrtana* as the best of all; they don't feel respect for it. Their respect is directed somewhere else. Such worldly fools are offenders of the Holy Names.

Śrī Sanātana Gosvāmin makes another point of the greatest importance in his *Bṛhad-bhāgavatāmṛta*. He has said: The direct vision of Kṛṣṇa

---

[38]Jīva's comm. on Bhāg. 11.5.32: यज्ञैः पूजासम्भारैः। न यत्र यज्ञेशमखा महोत्सवा इत्युक्तेः। तत्र विशेषेण तमेवाभिधेयं व्यनक्ति। सङ्कीर्तनं बहुभिर्मिलित्वा तद्गानसुखं श्रीकृष्णगानं तत्प्रधानैः। तथा सङ्कीर्तनप्राधान्यस्य तदाश्रितेष्वेव दर्शनात्स एव अभिधेय इति स्पष्टम्।

[39]Sanātana says: "lack of attentiveness towards the Holy Name is also a kind of offense." नाम्न्यनवधानताप्येकोऽपराधः

[40]Cc., 1.3.62-63:

> *saṅkīrtana-pravartak śrīkṛṣṇacaitanya*
> *saṅkīrtanayajñe tāñre bhaje sei dhanya*
> *sei to sumedhā, ār kubuddhi saṃsāra*
> *sarvayajña haite kṛṣṇanāmayajñasāra*

which is the highest goal of worship will not occur as long as one is not fully intent[41] on *kīrtana* of the Holy Names:

> For him only the direct vision of Śrī Madanagopāla remains [to be achieved]. Attachment to chanting (*japa*) is not what he needs; instead he needs attachment to *kīrtana* of his Names.[42]

In his commentary Sanātana has said: "Attachment to the *kīrtana* of the Holy Names, that is, having one's mind intently fixed on it is necessary, because only by that is it possible to see Madanagopāla [Kṛṣṇa] directly."[43]

Then in the next verse Sanātana says: "There is no better way of worshipping Śrī Madanagopāla than *saṅkīrtana* of names such as Kṛṣṇa, Gopāla, Govinda, and so forth, that is [no better way] than loud *kīrtana* of those names with melody, rhythm, and tempo."[44]

The statement "intently fixed on" in the commentary of verse 103 is particularly worthy of attention. Whatever form of *bhakti* one practices the mind should be intently fixed on the *saṅkīrtana* of the Holy Names. Where is the mind focused? — this is the big question. This indicates what one thinks is important.

The minds of Śrī Gaurahari and his companions were intent upon *saṅkīrtana* of the Holy Names. That is clear from their speech and behavior. Whatever form of worship of Śrī Gaurahari one undertakes, if *saṅkīrtana* of the Holy Names is not primary, he is not pleased with it. He does not accept it. Therefore in the *Bhāgavata* verse (11.5.32) it is said that one who keeps *saṅkīrtana* of the Holy Names as the main practice is wise; but Kṛṣṇadāsa Kavirāja calls foolish.anyone who does not keep it as the

---

[41] *Abhiniveśa* is the word in the original here. It means application towards, intentness on, study of, affection for, and devotion to some thing or someone. [Trans.]

[42] Bb., 2.1.103:

> केवलं तत्पदाम्भोजसाक्षादीक्षावशिष्यते।
> तज्जपेऽर्हति नासक्तिं किन्तु तन्नामकीर्तने॥

This verse is about a *brāhmaṇa* who came to Gopakumāra in search of guidance. Gopakumāra judges his level of advancement and recommends *kīrtana* of the Holy Names in order to achieve a vision of Madanagopāla (Kṛṣṇa). [Trans.]

[43] Bb., 2.1.103: तस्य श्रीमदनगोपालस्य तयोर्वा पदाम्भुजयोः साक्षादीक्षैवावशिष्टास्ति। तत्तस्मात्त-स्य श्रीमदनगोपालस्य नाम्नां कीर्तन एवासक्तिं चित्ताभिनिवेशमर्हति। तेनैव तत्सिद्धेः।

[44] Bb., 2.1.104-105.

main practice.[45] Therefore, understand what direction Mahāprabhu's [Śrī Gaurahari's] mind moved in, what he was intent upon.

Śrī Gaurahari was the father of *saṅkīrtana* of the Holy Names. [As Kavi Karṇapūra says:] "This is the creation of Śrī Kṛṣṇacaitanya."[46] A father's attention resides in the son above all else. What more can be said?

For Sanātana Gosvāmin, who has himself written the verse mentioned above in which it is said that as long as there is not full attention on the *saṅkīrtana* of the Holy Names one does not attain Kṛṣṇa, it is not necessary to say that his own attention was above all on the Holy Names. Therefore, he has described *saṅkīrtana* as his highest life, his greatest ornament and his fullest joy.[47]

About Rūpa Gosvāmin it is said: "All eight periods of the day he worships Kṛṣṇa, only sleeping an hour and a half. And, because of *saṅkīrtana* even that much [sleep] does not happen some days."[48] What attention on *saṅkīrtana*! Only an hour and a half for sleep and because of absorption in *saṅkīrtana* some days there is not even time for that.

Of Raghunātha Dāsa Gosvāmin it is [also] said:

> Day and night he does *saṅkīrtana*
> He does not leave his Lord's feet for one moment.
> Seven and a half periods he spends
> in *kīrtana* and remembering
> Only an hour and a half
> are for eating and sleeping
> and that too not every day.[49]

---

[45]Cc., 1.3.76-77.

[46]Kavi Karṇapūra, Ccn., 8.33: इयमियं भगवत्कृष्णचैतन्यसृष्टिः

[47]Sanātana, Bb., 1.1.9: परमममृतमेकं जीवनं भूषणं मे

[48]Cc., 2.19.118:

> *aṣṭaprahar kṛṣṇabhajan — cāridaṇḍa śayane*
> *nāmasaṅkīrtane seho nahe konodine*

[49]Cc., 3.6.250 and 3.6.304:

> *rātridina kare tiñho nāmasaṅkīrtan*
> *kṣaṇamātra nāhi chāḍe prabhur caraṇ*
> *sāḍe sātaprahar yāy kīrtane smaraṇe*
> *āhāranidrā cāridaṇḍa se nahe kono dine*

Śrī Raghunātha Dāsa Gosvāmin used to perform *saṅkīrtana* day and night. With what sort of attention? That can be known from one of his own verses:

> The name "Rādhā" is beautiful, fresh ambrosia; the name "Kṛṣṇa" is sweet, condensed milk. O thirsty tongue, make them even more pleasing each and every moment with the ice of fragrant attachment and drink deeply.[50]

This "ice of fragrant attachment" reveals the deep attachment in his mind for *saṅkīrtana*.

The great poet Kavi Karṇapūra was deeply intent on the Holy Name. The way he described the reaction of the wives of the *brāhmaṇas* on hearing the Holy Name reveals this:

> One 'Kṛṣṇa' spoken by the friends of Kṛṣṇa began to ring in their ears in a limitless number of forms. They lost all interest in carrying out the duties assigned to them. What is this *mantra* of enchantment? By the intense pull of this indescribable, unparalleled, amazing, inconceivable *mantra* of enchantment they all started down the path together like golden dolls or like does enchanted by a spell.[51]

Now, Laghu, you should search your own heart and see where, wittingly or unwittingly, your own attention lies. Are you unfortunately imbued with the preferences of meditating *yogīs* like Pippalāyana and others, or are you out of good fortune imbued with the preferences of our Gosvāmins?

---

[50] Raghunātha Dāsa, *Stavāvalī*:

> राधेति नाम नवसुन्दरसीधुमुग्धं
> कृष्णेति नाम मधुराद्भुतगाढदुग्धम् ।
> सर्वक्षणं सुरभिरागहिमेन रम्यं
> कृत्वा तदेव पिब मे रसने क्षुधार्ते॥

[51] Kavikarṇapūra, *Ānanda-vṛndāvana-campu*, 13.20.

Chapter 8

The Case of Ajāmila

Laghu: Very well. In the story of Ajāmila in the Sixth Canto, Second Chapter of the *Bhāgavata*, the objective is to reveal the astounding potency of the Holy Name through the logic of "how much more so."[1] Still, why do we see that the offenseless Ajāmila is not taken immediately to Vaikuṇṭha at the time of his death through his similative usage of the Holy Name to refer to another? Being taken to Vaikuṇṭha is the established conclusion according to the *Bhāgavata*:

> Anyone, even persons more animal than human, who at the time of death merely pronounces, purely or impurely, one name from among his many names (ie., Kṛṣṇa, Govinda, and so forth), becomes free immediately from sins accumulated over numerous lifetimes and attains the eternal, the conscious, and the joyful Lord. I seek shelter with that supreme being.[2]

---

[1] *Kaimutya-nyāya* — The logic of "how much more so" is often used to suggest the power or lack thereof of some thing or act. An example would be: This fire is hot enough to melt iron, how much more would a huge forest fire melt it. In this case the *kaimutya* is: "The Holy Name even as a semblance was able to deliver Ajāmila, who was only calling his own son. How much more will it deliver those who use it in earnest to call Kṛṣṇa.

[2] Bhāg., 3.9.15:

> यस्यावतारगुणकर्मविडम्बनानि
> नामानि येऽसुविगमे विवशा गृणन्ति।
> तेऽनेकजन्मशमलं सहसैव हित्वा
> संयान्त्यपावृतमृतं तमजं प्रपद्ये॥

The interpretation above is based on the commentaries of Śrī Jīva and Śrī Viśvanātha. Here is what they say. First Śrī Jīva: "By the words 'at the time of death' it is implied that the pronunciation of the Holy Name is mere pronunciation only without any motive or objective and that the syllables are impure [slurred or poorly pronounced]."[3] Thus he suggests in his commentary that this is a case of a semblance of the Holy Name (*nāmābhāsa*). And Viśvanātha: "Because, by means of a mere semblance of the Holy Name, without even the slightest hint of a sense of worship, he still gives his own realm to people who are more like animals than humans, the wonderment of the grace of the Holy Name is revealed here."[4] Why then for Ajāmila was there a delay?

Goswami When there is no offense, uttering the direct name of the Lord happens in two ways. It is either spoken without affection or with affection. What is attained by these is described below.

If one utters the Holy Name without affection once at the time of death, the Holy Name himself immediately causes that person to reach the Vaikuṇṭha realm. If one utters the Holy Name with affection he not only causes that person to reach Vaikuṇṭha, he brings that person close to himself for the purpose of service. The Lord himself has actively revealed many names and in them has placed as eternally present all of his powers. This Śrī Gaura has said in the second verse of his *Śikṣāṣṭaka* (Eight Stanzas of Instruction).[5]

Śrī Jīva in his *Krama-sandarbha* commentary on the *Bhāgavata* has even more clearly discussed this topic. He says:

> Therefore, when it is said that by performing worship and so forth only once one gets the result, it is true as long as there is no ancient or recent offense. But at death one must somehow or other offer worship at least once. In that case, someone who has performed, either in a previous life or in this life, worship of the Lord is certain to utter the name of the Lord, even if only once. In their case the Holy Name exerts its own influence and immediately such a person meets the Lord. The evidence for this is found in the *Bhagavad-gītā* (8.6):

---

[3]असुविगमेऽपीति तदानीन्तनतन्मात्रत्वमशुद्धवर्णत्वञ्च व्यञ्जितम्। विवशा इति तदिच्छां विना केनचित्कारणान्तरेणापीत्यर्थः।

[4]उक्तलक्षणोपास्योपासनाज्ञानगन्धमपि विना नामाभासमात्रत एव पशुतुल्येभ्योऽपि जनेभ्यः स्वपददायित्वेन परमकृपाश्चर्यमाचक्षाणः सविशेषस्वरूप एव स्वप्रपत्तिं विज्ञापयति यस्येति।

[5]नाम्नामकारि बहुधा निजसर्वशक्तिस्तत्रार्पिता नियमितः स्मरणे न कालः।

> "Whatever one remembers at the time of death, one attains to that after leaving behind the body." Therefore, because there is an absence of offense, there is no need for repeating the Holy Name over and over again in order to destroy it — as with Ajāmila.[6]

The evidence for what was said about attaining the Lord by uttering his name in two ways at the time of death is found in the *Bhāgavata*:

> [Śrī Kṛṣṇa addresses the cowherd women:] The *bhakti* for me that the living beings have makes them immortal. But, the affection that, by your good fortune, you have for me brings you to me.[7]

After presenting such a word of encouragement, he [Kṛṣṇa] immediately raises a "but." That "but" is spoken in the following verse, again from the *Bhāgavata*:

> But, though they worship me, I do not reveal myself to living beings in order to increase their attachment, eagerness, and longing for me. It is just like a poor person who, after finding a great treasure, has lost it. Consumed by the thought of it, he knows nothing else.[8]

---

[6] Jīva, comm. on Bhāg., 6.2.23: तदेव यत्सकृद्भजनादिनैव फलोदय उक्तस्तद्यथावदेव यदि प्राचीनोऽर्वाचीनो वापराधो न स्यात्। मरणे तु सर्वदा सकृदेव यथाकथञ्चिदपि भजनमपेक्षते। तत्र हि तस्यैव सकृदपि भगवन्नामग्रहणादिकं जायते यस्य पूर्वत्र वात्र वा जन्मनि सिद्धेन भगवदाराधनादिना तदानीं स्वीय प्रभावं प्रकटयतानन्तरमेव भगवत्साक्षात्कारो भाव्यते, यं यं वापि स्मरन् भावमिति श्रीगीतोपनिषद्भ्यः। ततोऽपराधाभावात्तत्क्षयार्थं तत्रावृत्त्यपेक्षा ... यथाजामिलस्य।

[7] Bhāg., 10.82.44:

मयि भक्तिर्हि भूतानाममृतत्वाय कल्पते।
दिष्ट्या यदासीन्मत्स्नेहो भवतीनां मदापनः॥

[8] Bhāg., 10.32.20:

नाहं तु सख्यो भजतोऽपि जन्तून्
भजाम्यमीषामनुवृत्तिवृत्तये।
यथाधनो लब्धधने विनष्टे
तच्चिन्तयान्यन्निभृतो न वेद॥

The second half of this verse is not included in Mani Babu's original text. I have added it because it is discussed in Śrī Jīva's following commentary. [Trans.]

In accordance with this statement of the Lord himself, he causes a delay in attaining him.[9]

In his commentary on *Bhāgavata*, Śrī Jīva says:

> [Kṛṣṇa says] "I once said: 'Nārada, I do not live in Vaikuṇṭha, nor in the heart of the *yogī*. Wherever my devotees are singing my names, that is where I am.' Even though I am wherever my devotees are singing my names in fulfillment of that promise, I am not visible to them. Cowherd women, this is my behavior towards all, not just towards you. Don't think that it is a sign of my indifference towards you." The cowherd women ask: "Why don't you appear to them?" Kṛṣṇa replies: "In order to increase their longing for me, that longing from which arises ceaseless meditation on me." The cowherd women respond: "But we are always in the highest state of love for you." Kṛṣṇa replies: "True. Still, it is to make that love even more special. The point is made by means of an example: 'like a poor person who has found wealth and then lost it.' By this example a special kind of distraction or total engagement of the mind is taught. Therefore, in order to keep them ceaselessly absorbed in thought of me, I do not show myself easily." Thus, there is no expectation for any kind of return because there is only dependence on love (*prema*) and because all goals are fulfilled through the all-subduing power of Kṛṣṇa's beauty, qualities, and so forth. Though he [Kṛṣṇa] is equal to a compassionate parent, that compassionate parenthood is transcended and his own well-wishing is revealed by his giving a love for himself that does not also bestow himself, but that brings him under control and that is the very crown jewel of all the goals of humankind. Moreover, the superiority of the tasting of the *rasa* [flavor] of love for the beloved is made known through Kṛṣṇa's desire to increase it ceaselessly and through the cowherd women's toleration of the pains of separation for that purpose.[10]

---

[9]Jīva, comm. on Bhāg., 6.2.23: इति तत्वाक्यदिशा विलम्बेन प्रापयति।

[10]Jīva, *Vaiṣṇava-toṣaṇī* on Bhāg., 10.32.20: नाहं वसामि वैकुण्ठे योगिनां हृदये न च। मद्भक्ता यत्र गायन्ति तत्र तिष्ठामि नारदेत्यादि मदुक्तिभिस्तन्निकटे स्थितमपि स्वं तेभ्यो न दर्शयामीत्यर्थः। नञः सर्वादौ प्रयोगः स्ववाक्येनैव स्वस्य यन्त्रनापत्त्या परमवैयग्र्यात्। हे सख्य इति आत्माराम-त्वादिराहित्यमेव साधितम्। जन्तूनित्यवशेषात्सर्वत्रैवेदृशो मम व्यवहारो न तु भवतीष्वेवेति नात्मनि ममोदासीन्यं शङ्कनीयमिति भावः। कथं न भजसि? तत्राह अमीषामिति अनुवृत्तीनां निरन्तरध्यानानां

In this way the reason for somewhat of a delay in attaining the Lord even when there is no offense has been shown in general. Now, from the perspective of demonstrated conclusion, an answer will be given to the present question: "Why was there a delay for Ajāmila?"

> Ajāmila felt affection towards the name Nārāyaṇa because of his relationship with his son named Nārāyaṇa. But, he had no connection with the Lord of Vaikuṇṭha named Nārāyaṇa. On the other hand, the Lord [Nārāyaṇa], who was fond of his name, is seen to be deeply identified with his name. For that reason, when Ajāmila called out "Nārāyaṇa" to his son at the time of his death, the Lord's compassionate glance fell upon him. Along with that, the Lord's companions, too, felt great respect for Ajāmila. Though Ajāmila had spoken his name with affection, the Lord wanted to bring him to himself after giving him the highest kind of affection through *kīrtana* that is preceded by a feeling of intense longing for the Name. Knowing this, the Lord's companions did not immediately bring him into their company.[11]

In this way the incomprehensible, amazing power of the syllables of the Holy Name has been shown. The syllables of the Holy Name even without being connected with the Holy Named are able to give all success. This is so because *ekameva ... tattvaṃ dvidhāvirbhūtam,* "the one truth has appeared as two, as the Holy Name and the Holy Named." Śrī Jīva in his commentary on *Bhāgavata,* 6.2.20, has revealed another teaching that confirms one given earlier in this discussion. Those who are single-form devotees, fully engaged in *saṅkīrtana* of the Holy Names without dependence on any thing else, even if they do not reach out prematurely for the remembering form of *bhakti,* will be caught up by remembering, like being possessed by a ghost, when the time is right

---

वृत्तिर्यस्मात्तस्मै सन्ततप्रेमप्रकर्षायेत्यर्थः। नन्वस्माकं त्वय्यनुवृत्तिवृत्तिः सदा वर्तत एवेति चेत्सत्यं तथापि वैशिष्ट्यार्थमिति सदृष्टान्तमाह यथेति। विशेषतो नष्टे हारित इति वैयग्र्यविशेषो दर्शितः। अतएव तच्चिन्तया नितरां भृतो व्याप्तः। तदेवं रूपगुणादिना सर्ववशित्वात्सर्वार्थपूर्णत्वेन प्रेममात्रसापेक्षत्वेन च प्रत्युपकाराणपेक्षतया साम्येऽपि करुणपितॄनप्यतिक्रम्य स्वस्य हितैषित्वं दर्शितं स्वादेयस्ववशीकारसर्वपुरुषार्थशिरोमणिस्वप्रेमदानात्। तथा प्रियप्रेमरसास्वादाधिक्यं च बोधितं सन्ततत‌द्वर्धनलालसात्तदर्थं तद्विरहदुःखसहनाच्चेति ज्ञेयम्।

[11] Jīva, Ks, on 6.2.20: तदेवं सत्यजामिलोऽप्ययमारोपिततन्नाम्नः पुत्रस्य सम्बन्धेन तन्नाम्न्यपि स्निह्यति स्म तस्मिन्स्वनाम्नि श्रीभगवतोऽप्यभिमानः सान्द्रो दृश्यते यतस्तद्विषया मतिरित्यत्र। यतः पार्षदानामपि महानेव तत्रादरो दृष्टस्तस्मात्स्नेहसम्बलनया गृहीतस्वनाम्नि सत्यपि तस्मिन्नुत्कण्ठापूर्वकसाक्षान्निजकीर्तनादिद्वारा साक्षान्निजस्नेहं प्रकृष्टं दत्त्वा तं नेतुमिच्छति प्रभुरिति ज्ञात्वा सहसा नात्मभिः सह तं नीतवन्त इति सर्वं समञ्जसम्॥

and when it is proper for them. Since a deep identification of the Lord of Goloka, the Sportful Best of Persons, the Holy Named, resides in his Names, his compassionate glance falls on those who perform *saṅkīrtana* of the Holy Names. This Lord, the Holy Named, by his own choice and by his own grace causes remembering and all the other forms of *bhakti* to appear in the heart of his devotee at the right time and as the need arises. Then he leads the single-form devotee to the highest stage of longing and fulfills him by giving him direct service to perform in the bower.[12]

Thus has Śrī Jīva explained the reason for the delay in Ajāmila's attainment of Kṛṣṇa after uttering once at the time of his death the name "Nārāyaṇa" as a semblance of the Holy Name. While discussing that Śrī Jīva, at the end of his commentary, has given us a peek into the process of worship and of attaining of Kṛṣṇa in the words "through *kīrtana* that is preceded by a feeling of intense longing for the Name." From the time that Ajāmila named his son Nārāyaṇa, whenever he called his son by that name his son was in his mind in such a way that his affection for his son was infused into the syllables of that name. His mind had no connection with the Nārāyaṇa who is the Lord of Vaikuṇṭha. Even so, by that one semblance of the Holy Name appearing on the lips of sinless and offenseless Ajāmila at the time of his death, the Named One, Nārāyaṇa, the Lord of Vaikuṇṭha, accepted him as one of his own and determined to give him the highest taste and the joy of service. The way he fulfilled that determination is shown in the last portion of Śrī Jīva's commentary.

One has to reconcile the teachings of the two verses cited before, "The *bhakti* for me ..." and "But, though they are worshiping me ..." with the case of Ajāmila being discussed here. For instance, the cowherd women's affection for Kṛṣṇa was first raised to the level of intense longing and then they saw him again. Therefore in Ajāmila's case his affection for the syllables of the name "nārāyaṇa" was first raised to the level of intense longing and then after performing *kīrtana* and other practices directly connected with Nārāyaṇa, he meets him. The meaning of the words *tasmin utkaṇṭhāpūrvaka* in Jīva's commentary is "preceded by intense longing for the syllables of the name Nārāyaṇa." They cannot be understood according to any other meaning, example, or context. Remember, the context of this *Bhāgavata* verse is the demonstration of the

[12]The "bower" is a reference to the confidential or intimate service of Rādhā and Kṛṣṇa in a forest bower in which they secretly meet outside their villages.

incomprehensible and amazing power of the Holy Name by showing the greatness of its mere semblance using the logic of "how much more so" (*kaimutya*). People are encouraged thereby to perform *kīrtana* of the Holy Names.

Ajāmila's process of worship leading to his final meeting with the Lord went like this:

Stage One: Semblance of the Holy Name.

↓

Stage Two: Affection invested in the syllables of the Holy Name.

↓

Stage Three: Intense longing evoked by the syllables of the Holy Name.

↓

Stage Four: Direct *kīrtana* of Nārāyaṇa impelled by intense longing.

↓

Stage Five: Fully developed affection for Nārāyaṇa through *kīrtana*

↓

Stage Six: Meeting with Kṛṣṇa and the tasting of sweetness.

Take note: In Stage One, the semblance of the Holy Name is the application of the name of Nārāyaṇa to someone else. The affection (*sneha*) referred to in Stage Two is the result of a maturing or ripening of love[13] and in Ajāmila's case was directed to his son. In Stage Three that affection is elevated to intense longing and the syllables of the Holy Name become the subject of recollection or meditations. In Stage Four the focus is fully switched from son to Lord Nārāyaṇa, the Lord of Vaikuṇṭha. In Stage Five Ajāmila gradually begins to remember the forms, qualities, and sports of Nārāyaṇa and an intense desire to see the Lord of Vaikuṇṭha appears.[14] He thinks "I can no longer remain without seeing him." And finally comes the stage of Ajāmila's meeting with the Lord.

Living beings who are offenders of the Holy Name, however, follow a different process. Ajāmila's natural affection (*sneha*) was first for his son, the one named Nārāyaṇa. Later it was transferred to the name Nārāyaṇa. An offending living being, however, first of all comes in contact with *kīrtana* of the Holy Name. Here his connection is directly with the Lord, not with any other thing. Here too the destruction of offenses

---

[13] Jīva, Vt. on Bhāg., 10.82.44.

[14] Jīva, Vt. on Bhāg. 10.32.10

depends on the *kīrtana* of the Holy Name. After the offenses are destroyed the living being first begins to remember the Holy Name and then later the forms, qualities and sports. To reach the level of affection a lot of practice or cultivation is needed. All of this will occur according to the process delineated in the first verse of Śrī Gaura's own eight verses of instruction:

> *Saṅkīrtana* of the Names of Kṛṣṇa cleanses the mirror of the mind, puts out the great forest fire of the ills of worldly becoming, spreads moonlight on the lily of the highest good (love for Kṛṣṇa) causing it to blossom, brings life to the wife of wisdom (the *bhakti* of love), increases the ocean of joy, makes one taste the richest ambrosia at every step and bathes the whole self with joy. May it be supremely victorious.[15]

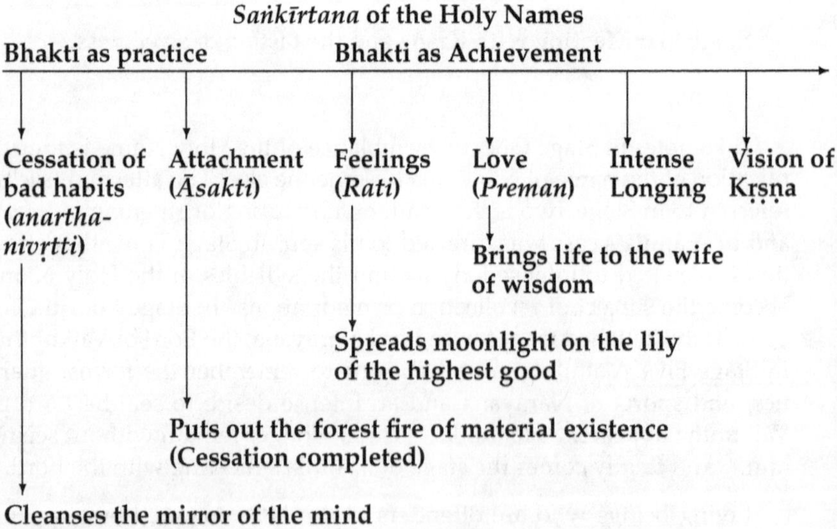

---

[15] Śrī Caitanya, Śa, 1:

चेतोदर्पणमर्जनं भवमहादावाग्निनिर्वापनम्
श्रेयःकैरवचन्द्रिकावितरनं विद्यावधूजीवनम्।
आनन्दाम्बुधिवर्धनं प्रतिपदं पूर्णामृतास्वादनम्
सर्वात्मस्नपनं परं विजयते श्रीकृष्णसङ्कीर्तनम्॥

According to the process described, after practicing for a while one reaches the stage where one's undesirable habits and tendencies are nearly stopped but love has not been born. One then reaches a state of mind in which he thinks "Durn! All of the efforts I have made and they have all turned out fruitless. Not even a little of Kṛṣṇa's grace has been bestowed on such an offender as me. To hell with me." In this way, through the steady increase of remorse and wretchedness, lust and anger disappear and *bhakti* increases until it becomes set ablaze. After that, for those whose love is now born, in order to keep their "following" (*anuvṛtti*) or attachment to Kṛṣṇa alive [Kṛṣṇa says] "I do not submit to them." That is, though he may give them a brief vision of himself, he withdraws that vision. By this their attachment assumes a very powerful form and those devotees whose love is awakened become like those poor people who have found but then lost great wealth.[16]

[16]Viśvanātha, comm. on Bhāg., 10.32.20: हन्त हन्त यमेवोद्यमं करोमि स एव विफली भवति तस्मान्मय्यपराधिन्यनुग्रहलेशोऽपि कृष्णस्य नास्ति धिङ्मामिति प्रतिक्षणं निर्वेददैन्यादिवृद्धा कामक्रो-धाद्यपगमैर्भक्तिः प्रदीप्तीभवत्यजातप्रेम्नाम्। जातप्रेम्नां तु अनुवृत्तिर्मदासक्तिस्तस्या जीविकार्थं न भजामि दर्शनं दत्त्वाप्यन्तर्दधामि तत एवानुवृत्तिरासक्तिः प्रवृद्धीभवति।

Chapter 9

Kali and the Eighth Offense

Laghu: Okay, previously, in your discussion of the offenses to the Holy Name, you said that thinking that auspicious actions were equal to the Holy Names was the eighth offense. What do you mean in that case by auspicious actions?

Goswami:

> Victory, victory to the blissful name of Murāri which ends the drudgery of following one's own *dharma*, of meditation, of performing rites of worship and so forth; that name, if somehow uttered even once, gives liberation to living beings. It is my greatest nectar, my very life, my only adornment.[1]

We are being cheated out of tasting the joy of the Holy Name, which was the highest life, the highest joy and the highest adornment of Śrī

---

[1]Sanātana Gosvāmin, Bb., 1.1.9:

> जयति जयति नामानन्दरूपं मुरारे-
> र्विरमितनिजधर्मपूजादियत्नं।
> कथमपि सकृदात्तं मुक्तिदं प्राणिनां यत्
> परमममृतमेकं जीवनं भूषणं मे॥

Sanātana, by the onslaught of the injustice of king Kali.[2]

> The path of *bhakti* is blocked by millions of thorns in the form of the Age of Kali and the powerful, inimical senses."[3]

At the completion of five hundred years from the appearance of Śrī Gaura, Kali departs and the age of love, of pure goodness, arrives.[4] Time is short. In the meantime king Kali must wrap up his affairs and get out. Therefore, all the hustle and bustle. We have fallen at present into his deadly bite. Kali's teeth or rather his primary weapons are the ten offenses. Among those again his "brahma-weapon"[5] or most powerful weapon is the eighth offense: "considering auspicious actions like *dharma*, vows, and so forth to be equal to the Holy Names." Even though here the forms of *bhakti* too have been included in auspicious actions as primary, by the trickery of Kali an error occurs right there through inattentiveness. To take whomever is the best of all, seated on the throne like a great emperor, and pull him off of that throne and make him sit on one seat alongside the generals, the village policemen and so forth is certainly not showing respect to that king. That is disrespect — that is an offense. Out of fear of that kind of offense Sūta Goswami shivered when he recounted the source of all descents (*avatārī*), Śrī Kṛṣṇa, together with all of his descents (*avatāra*). Therefore, he quickly raised him up with

---

[2]The Age of Kali (One, Quarrel) personified. See the glossary for a discussion of the Hindu system of ages

[3]Prabodhānanda Sarasvatī, *Caitanya-candrāmṛta*, verse 47:

> कालः कलिर्बलिन इन्द्रियवैरिवर्गाः
> भक्तिमार्ग इह कण्टककोटिरुद्धः ।

[4]This is an idea put forward by Manindranath's guru, Śrī Kanupriya Goswami. It was first broached in an essay written in 1929 for a monthly journal called *Sonār Gaurāṅga* (Golden Gaurāṅga or the Golden Golden One). That essay has been translated into English as *The Dawn of the Age of Love.* He says: "When Kali leaves this time, there will be the appearance of an extraordinary period in human history — up until the time of the Satya Yuga [427,000 years hence]. The religion of ecstatic love placed in the world by Śrī Gaurāṅga Mahāprabhu will gradually expand its influence over the whole world and engaging all mankind in one religion, inspiring them with a common spirit and a common purpose, will submerge the entire world in an unprecedented flood of astounding *prema*. ... We can also call it the 'prema yuga.'" (p. 51)

[5]*Brahmāstra* (aka. *brahma-śiras*), the "brahma-weapon" is a mythological weapon, an arrow empowered by mantra, that figures in the *Mahābhārata* story and its reflection in the First Canto of the *Bhāgavata Purāṇa*. It is the weapon used by Aśvatthāman, son of Droṇa, to attempt to destroy the last remaining Pāṇḍavas after the end of the great war. See *Mahābhārata*, Book 10, Chapters 12-16.

the highest respect and seated him on his own sovereign seat with the statement "but Kṛṣṇa is the Lord himself."[6] Then he felt peace.

> He gave the general characteristics of all descents.
> And among them Kṛṣṇacandra was counted.
> Then Sūta Goswami felt a great fear in his heart.
> Those whose characteristics he specified,
> they are all descents — parts and portions of the Person (*Puruṣsa*).
> Kṛṣṇa, though, is himself the lord, the crown of all.[7]

Sūta Gosāi did not have just an ordinary fear. He had a 'great fear.' Why a great fear? The biggest obstacle to attaining the feet of Śrī Kṛṣṇa is that offense. Therefore, he was greatly afraid. The Holy Name and the Holy Named are in all ways non-different, in majesty and in sweetness. Therefore, what is said in the case of the Named is said in the case of the Name. The Holy Name is the source or the whole, the seed. All of the other forms of worship are its supporting forms. All the other forms of worship come out of this one source. "That which is above and beyond all the others, that is the source or the whole; and that which nourishes or supports the source, that is the part."[8] Thus, thinking that a part is equal to the whole, the seed, the best of all, is an offense. This is the eighth offense. Though Sūta Gosāi was very fearful, by Kali's trickery we are not frightened at all.

If we are to get beyond this trickery of Kali we have to understand well Śrī Jīva's commentary on this eighth offense and hold it in our hearts like a mantra-charged talisman. The eighth offense is presented thus in the *Padma Purāṇa*: "Thinking *dharma*, vows, renunciation, sacrifices and other kinds of auspicious acts to be the equal to the Holy Name

---

[6]कृष्णस्तु भगवान् स्वयम्।

[7]Cc., 1.2.68-70:

> *sab avatārer kari sāmānya lakṣaṇ*
> *tār madhye kṛṣṇacandra karila gaṇan*
> *tabe sūta gosāi mane pāñā baḍa bhaya*
> *yār ye lakṣaṇa tā karila niścaya*
> *avatār sab — puruṣer kalā aṃśa*
> *kṛṣṇa svayaṃ bhagavān sarva abataṃsa*

[8]Rūpa, Brs., 4.8.42:

> सोऽङ्गी सर्वातिगो यः ... स एवाङ्गं भवेदङ्गिपोषि

is an offense to the Holy Name."[9] Here Kali creates mistaken notions in relationship to the words *dharma* and "auspicious acts" (*śubhakriyā*). The conventional view holds that *dharma* here means practices from the ritual and knowledge portions of the Veda, such as the worship of the gods and goddesses, sacrifices and so forth. The forms of *bhakti* are not to be included in those. Moreover, "auspicious acts" does not mean *bhakti* either because *bhakti* does not fall in the division of actions [it is a feeling or mental state].

In response to that opposing view Śrī Jīva says in his commentary on the eighth offense:

> Thinking that *dharma* and the rest are equal to the Name of Hari is an offense. For this reason it is said [in the *Padma purāṇa*] that each and every Name of Viṣṇu is greater than all the Vedas.[10]

Here the second half of this statement [the Name is greater than the Vedas, greater than everything] is what is to be proven or the effect, and the first half [thinking *dharma* and such are equal to the Name is an offence] is the proof or material cause. The citation from the *Padma Purāṇa* is the instrumental cause. If by *dharma* the [mundane] actions of the ritual and knowledge portions of the Veda was meant, then, with those as one's material cause, how can one prove anything pertaining to the non-material world?

If one takes clay in hand as one's material cause, can one create an effect like a gold pot? One can't. The effect and the cause have to be of the same kind. Therefore, here *dharma* must certainly refer to consciousness or spiritual *dharma* and thus to *bhakti*. Śrī Jīva has many times in other places given *bhakti* as the main meaning of *dharma*. To make this matter even more easily understood I will expand a little more on it. The point Śrī Jīva wants to establish is that among all forms of *bhakti* the Holy Name is the best. The proof is that considering *dharma*, vows and other auspicious acts to be equal to the Holy Name is an offense. The proof text would be easy for everyone to understand, if it were put like this: "Considering the other forms of *bhakti* to be equal to the Holy Name is an offense." Since that is not the case one has to establish it by discussion

---

[9] Hbv., 11.523: धर्मव्रतत्यागहुतादिसर्वशुभक्रियासाम्यमपि प्रमादः

[10] Jīva, Ks., 2.1.11: धर्मादिभिः साम्यमननमपि प्रमादोऽपराधो भवतीत्यर्थः। अतएव पाद्मे (उ. 96.26) रामाष्टोत्तरशतनामस्तोत्रे विष्णोरेकैकनामापि सर्ववेदाधिकं मतमिति।

of scripture. Why is *bhakti* not included when one says "auspicious acts in the form of *dharma*?"

When a teacher says in class: "Iron is heavier than water (*jala*)," the question arises: "Your evidence, sir?" The teacher then cites evidence from material science: "Iron (Fe) is heavier than H2O." Here, since H2O and water refer to the same thing, the teacher's erudition is revealed. Otherwise, it would not be. In that very same way, since the thing referred to by the word *dharma* in the passage cited from the *Padma Purāṇa* as evidence is the same as that referred to by the word *Veda* in the point to be established, the most learned Śrī Jīva's erudition is revealed. There is no error, confusion or desire to mislead in his statement. In this way by the word *dharma* one means Veda. Thus, the conclusion is that thinking the Veda is equal to the Name of Hari is the eighth offense. And in mentioning the Veda one also includes the main form of *bhakti*, association with (i.e., listening to) the *Bhāgavata Purāṇa*. Therefore, from Śrī Jīva's commentary on the eighth offense it is clearly established that considering any of the other forms of *bhakti* to be equal to the Holy Name is an offense to the Holy Name.

Now let's consider the "auspicious acts" part of the statement "auspicious acts in the form of *dharma*." The words "auspicious acts" are generally used in relationship to the performance of rites of worship, festivals, sacrifices, funerary rites, marriage rites and so forth. By hearing it repeatedly we have grown so accustomed to thinking of it in this way that as soon as we hear it again that is what comes to mind. That *bhakti* too is an act or rite does not come to mind — this is the source of the mistake of the conventional view mentioned before. That *bhakti* is also included in the "auspicious acts" is ascertained in accordance with scripture. Take for instance when Śrī Rūpa in defining *bhakti* says "the favorable cultivation of Kṛṣṇa" (Brs., 1.1.11: *ānukūlyena kṛṣṇānuśīlanam*). Śrī Jīva in his commentary says:

> Just as the meaning of the verbal root ($\sqrt{kṛ}$, to do) of the word *kriyā* (act or action or rite) is meant [when it is used] so too is the meaning of the verbal root ($\sqrt{śīl}$, to act, to do, to practice) of the word *anuśīlana* (cultivation) implied. This has both an active and inactive side. The first is in the form of physical, verbal and mental action.[11]

[11] Jīva, comm. on Brs., 1.1.11: अनुशीलनमत्र क्रियाशब्दवद्धात्वर्थमात्रमुच्यते ... कायवाङ्मानसीयस्तच्चेष्टारूपा ।

From this it is understood that *bhakti* is an action and without doubt it is also auspicious. Therefore, the conclusion is that *bhakti* is included within auspicious acts.

One can understand in what sense Śrī Jīva has used the word *dharma* by observing his usage of the word in different places in his writings. Take for instance his commentary on *Bhāgavata* (11.19.27): "*Dharma* is said to be the production of *bhakti* for me."[12] He says:

> That by which *bhakti* for me is produced is called *dharma* in the fullest sense, nothing else. In other words, that is what *dharma* means in its primary sense. In this way, in a place where the word *bhakti* is used, the word *dharma* may also be used.[13]

Moreover, "Hey, best of the best of the twice-born, your *dharma* is the one approved by the ancients."[14] Śrī Jīva in his commentary on this verse says: "[Approved by the ancients means] approved by the original twelve teachers of *bhakti*, headed by Nārada, as well as by your own contemporary teacher. In this way *dharma* has purity."[15] Therefore, it is understood from the commentary that the word *dharma* has been used here to refer to pure *bhakti*, because pure *bhakti* and *dharma* primarily refer to the same thing.

Also, in Śrī Jīva's commentary on the *Bhāgavata* verse (1.1.2) "*Dharma*, free of all deceit, ...," he says "*dharma* is defined as *bhakti*."[16] In this way with many examples it can be shown that Śrī Jīva has everywhere taken *dharma* in the sense of *bhakti*. And he has also clearly said that that is not only *dharma*'s primary meaning, but that there is no other meaning. Therefore, here too he has taken the word *dharma* in its most natural and familiar way and given the citation from the *Padma Purāṇa*.

Finally, Laghu, you should keep in mind the proposition that is accepted by all that "the best path is the one taken by the great ones" and the teaching given by the example of Sūta Gosāi (Goswami) himself.

---

[12]Bhāg., 11.19.27: धर्मो मद्भक्तिकृत्प्रोक्तः

[13]Jīva, Ks., on 11.19.27: मद्भक्तिकृदेव धर्मः प्रकर्षेणोक्तो नान्यः ततः स एव मुख्यवृत्त्या धर्मशब्देन वाच्य इत्यर्थः। एवमेव भक्तावपि धर्मशब्दः।

[14]Bhāg., 10.52.30: द्विजोत्तमश्रेष्ठ धर्मस्ते वृद्धसम्मतः

[15]Jīva, Vt. on Bhāg. 10.52.30: वृद्धानां प्राचीनद्वादशभक्तानामाधुनिकस्वगुरुप्रभृतीनां च सम्मत इति धर्मस्य तावच्छुद्धता वर्तत एव।

[16]Jīva, Vt., on 1.1.2: धर्मोऽत्र श्रीभक्तिलक्षणः।

In accordance with that you should refrain from thinking of the Holy Name, which is the best of all forms of *bhakti*, the very source and seed of all those other forms, as equal to all those that are meant to support it. Then, with great respect and full awareness of its superiority, you should establish Lord Holy Name, like the king of kings, on the throne of your heart and serve him there. Your life's full happiness will then appear. If you protect yourself from this eighth offense and enter into the sheltering fortress of the Holy Name, Kali will no longer be able to touch you. The other nine offenses to the Holy Name will no longer occur in your life because the Holy Name himself will protect you. He vows to protect those who seek shelter with him. "My devotee is not destroyed."[17]

[17] न मे भक्तः प्रणश्यति

Chapter 10

One Last Doubt

Laghu: Very well, Śrī Sanātana has stated in various places that *saṅkīrtana* of the Holy Name is the best of all, that it is independent of all else and that it is the most intimate way of cultivating the love of Vraja. How can we reconcile those statements with the following passage of the *Caitanya-caritāmṛta*?

> Here is the essential meaning of the fourth verse.
> He has descended in order to spread
> love (*prema*) and the Holy Name.
> This purpose is true, but it is external.
> Listen, there is another more intimate intent.[1]

Here haven't love and the Holy Name been called external?

Goswami: Look, even though the *Caitanya-caritāmṛta* is written in Bengali verse it is an extremely deep work. You should not construe its meaning in such a haphazard fashion. You will fall into difficulty. First try to understand a little something before you speak.

[1] Cc., 1.4.4-5:

caturtha śloker artha ei kaila sār
prema nāma pracārite ei abatār
satya ei hetu kintu eho bahiraṅga
ār ek hetu śon āche antaraṅga

Very well then, listen. In this passage "external" (*bahirannga*) means secondary (*gauṇa*).[2] What is secondary? The *spreading* of love and the Holy Name. This spreading is what is secondary, not love and the Holy Name. External or secondary are not the modifiers of love and the Holy Name; they modify spreading.

Okay, now why is this spreading of love and the Holy Name secondary? The answer to that is in a following verse of the *Caitanya-caritāmṛta*, Chapter Four: "incidental work, the killing of demons."[3] Kṛṣṇa's killing of demons was incidental or secondary — that work is done by the ordinary descents in the various ages — but the main reason for his coming was enjoyment of the sports of love with his own companions. In that same way, the incidental reason for Gaura's coming was the spreading of the *dharma* of the age, [namely] love and the Holy Name. However, that could have been done by any descent of the age. Rather, the main reason for his coming was to taste *rasa* with his dear companions. What *rasa* was that *rasa*? That is found in verse thirty-five of that same passage:

> For two reasons he descended with his devotees.
> He wished to taste for himself
> love and *saṅkīrtana* of the Holy Names.
> By that he infused even Caṇḍālas with *kīrtana*
> and stringing a garland of love and Holy Names
> he put it on the world.[4]

In his commentary on this verse, Viśvanātha Cakravartin said:

> The cause of Śrī Gaurahari's descent was tasting love and the Holy Names and by that infusing love. The reason for giving only two reasons here is that the third reason, experiencing the greatness of Rādhā's love, is included in tasting

---

[2]Viśvanātha: बहिरन्ङ्गः गौणः, अन्तरन्ङ्गः प्रधानः
[3]Cc., 1.4.13.
[4]Cc., 1.4.35-6:

> *dui hetu abatari lañā bhaktagaṇ*
> *āpane āsvāde premanāmasaṅkīrtan*
> *sei dvāre ācaṇḍāle kīrtana sañcāre*
> *nāmaprema mālā gānthi parāila saṃsāre*

> love. Therefore only the one reason, tasting love, has been mentioned. [5]

Therefore, it is seen that he tasted the *rasa* of love and *saṅkīrtana* of the Holy Names. The swelling up and overflowing of the ocean of love that took place in the circle dance on the bank of the Yamunā in Vṛndāvana manifested its form in the house of Śrīvāsa in Navadvīpa in the sweet *saṅkīrtana* of the Holy Names and in the manifestations of love of Śrī Gaurahari surrounded by his devotees.

> Is this bliss in physical form? The highest love in a body? Or, is this faith and compassion incarnate? Is this sweetness itself incarnate or the nine types of *bhakti* joined together in one body? No! This is Vakreśvara, equal to Gaurahari in trance, intoxicated by the blossoming of joy, dancing.[6]

Again the sounds of "Victory! Victory" arise in tumultuous joy. Oh, what a spectacle!

> Vakreśvara dances and Gaura claps and sweetly sings;
> then Vakreśvara sings and Gaura dances.
> Each experiences equal joy.[7]
> Flooding the world with a torrent of joy, the rain-cloud Gaura dances in front. His thundering roars make his followers dance like peacocks. The powerful downpour of his tears drench the earth. His shimmering physical radiance brighten up the world in all directions like flashes of lightning.[8]

---

[5]Viśvanātha, comm. on Cc., 1.4.35-26: श्रीचैतन्यावतारेऽपि मुख्यहेतुद्वयमाह दुइ हेतु इति। तत्र आत्मना नामप्रेमास्वादनं तद्द्वारेण च नामसङ्कीर्तनप्रेमसञ्चार इतिद्वयं तदवतारे हेतुः। यत्तु श्रीराधायाः प्रणयमहिमा इति अत्र हेतुत्रयमुक्तं तदपि आस्वाद्यत्वेन प्रेमास्वादनान्तर्भूतीकृत्य प्रेमास्वादनमेक एव हेतुरुक्तः।

[6]Kavikarṇapūra, *Caitanya-candrodaya Nāṭaka* (Ccn), 4.14:

आनन्द किमु मूर्त एष परमः प्रेमैव किं देहवान्
श्रद्धा मूर्तिमती दयैव किमु वा भुमौ स्वरूपिण्यसौ।
माधुर्यं नु शरीरि किं नवधा भक्तिर्गतैकां तनुं
तुल्यावेशसुखोत्सवो भगवता वक्रेश्वरो नृत्यति॥

[7]ibid., 4.15:

वक्रेश्वरे नृत्यति गौरचन्द्रो गायत्यमन्दं करतालिकाभिः।
वक्रेश्वरो गायति गौरचन्द्रे नृत्यत्यसौ तुल्यसुखानुभूतिः॥

[8]ibid., 4.16:

Again the wonderful variety of this ocean of *rasa* is seen in Gambhīrā in Purī, in the loud *saṅkīrtana* of Śrī Gaurahari, ecstatic in the tasting of the *rasa* of love-in-separation:

> At the door of Gambhīrā Govinda slept.
> The entire night he [Gaura] was awake,
> doing *saṅkīrtana* of the Holy Names,
> Suddenly the Master heard the sound of Kṛṣṇa's flute.
> In deep emotion the Master chased after it.[9]

In his *Caitanya-candrāmṛta*, Śrī Prabodhānanda Sarasvatī has glowingly described what condition the general populace was in, taught by the instructions of the father of *saṅkīrtana*, Śrī Gaurahari:

> Then in each and every house the tumultous sounds of *saṅkīrtana* of Hari arose and in each and every body, tears, trembling, goosebumps and the other eight appeared.[10]

Is it necessary to tell a woman who has just lost her husband "you should cry loudly now?" Rather, unable to keep herself from it, she begins to cry loudly on her own. In that same way a devotee who has reached the level of love becomes unsettled from the pain of separation from Kṛṣṇa and calls out "Kṛṣṇa, Kṛṣṇa" on his or her own.[11] That

---

गभीरैर्हुङ्कारैर्निजजनगणान्बर्हिणयति
द्रुतैर्बाष्पाम्भोभिर्भुवनमनिशं दुर्दिनयति।
महःपूरैर्विद्युद्दलयति दिक्षु प्रमदय-
न्नसौ विश्वं विश्वम्भरजलधरो नृत्यति पुरः॥

[9]Cc., 3.17.8:

gambhīrār dvāre govinda karila śayan
sab rātri jāgi kare saṅkīrtan
ācambite śune prabhu kṛṣṇa-veṇu-gān
bhābābeśe prabhu karila prayāṇ

[10]Prabodhānanda Sarasvatī, *Caitanya-candrāmṛta*, 30 :

अभूद्गेहे गेहे तुमुलहरिसङ्कीर्तनरवो
बभौ देहे देहे विपुलपुलकाश्रुव्यतिकरः।

[11]Sanātana, Bb., 2.3.167:

नाम्नां तु सङ्कीर्तनमार्तिभारान्मेघं विना प्रावृषि चातकानाम्।
रात्रौ वियोगात्स्वपते रथाङ्गीवर्गस्य चाक्रोशनवत्प्रतीहि।

is the defining characteristic of someone who has "arrived." And again "what characterizes the person who is successful the practitioner should practice." According to this line of reasoning the *saṅkīrtana* of the Holy Names of the Lord in beautiful, sweet songs and compositions, filled with feelings of deep pining, is to be performed by all practitioners. That is the intended meaning of all scriptures.[12]

Jaya Rādhe!

[12] ibid., comm. on Bb., 2.3.167: एवं परमार्त्या विचित्रमधुरगाथाप्रबन्धेन भगवन्नामसङ्कीर्तनं कार्यमिति तात्पर्यम्। सिद्धस्य लक्षणं यत्स्यात्साधनं साधकस्य तदिति न्यायात्।

Glossary of Terms and Names

ābhāsa Reflection or resemblance. This word is usually used at the end of compounds with other words to indicate that something is like something else or resembles something else. Thus, though it has never been used this way, *Elvis-ābhāsa* would mean "Elvis impersonator." It is most often used in this book with *nāma*, holy name. *Nāmābhāsa* is thus a "semblance of the holy name," It describes the case when a name of Kṛṣṇa is applied to someone else. Most Hindu Indians born in traditional families (and this is probably true of Muslim Indians, too, except using the names of Allah) are given the names of the various Hindu gods. Thus, Bankim Chandra Chatterjee, the famous Bengali writer of the 19th century, was given a colloquial, Bengali name of Kṛṣṇa, "Bent Moon." Any of the names of Kṛṣṇa when used to call or address anyone besides Kṛṣṇa are considered *nāmābhāsa* or "semblances of the holy name." The importance of this idea is found in the Vaiṣṇava belief that even in its semblance condition, the holy name can bring to the one who calls it liberation from the cycle of repeated birth and death.

For some *nāmābhasa* has another meaning in the theology of the holy name. For them, it also has come to mean the stage just before or at the very beginning of the full appearance of the holy name on the tongue of the aspiring Vaiṣṇava practitioner. In this sense it is compared with the first rays (*ābhāsa*) of the sun as it rises at the beginning of day. Thus, it indicates a stage in the development of the practitioner in which he or she has become nearly completely purified by practice and thus is "illumined" by the holy name to a greater degree than at the beginning of the spiritual practice.

This view is suggested by a verse from the *Padma Purāṇa* that is cited in Rūpa Gosvāmin's *Bhakti-rasāmṛtra-sindhu* (2.1.103). Such a view is also suggested by one of the auspicious opening verses of Lakṣmīdhara's *Śrī Bhagavan-nāma-kaumudī* (Moonlight on the Name of the Lord). This is not, however, semblance of the holy name in its technical sense (as the use of the holy name in reference to someone other than the holy named). It is more properly referred to as the "beginning of the rising of the holy name" (*nāmodayārambha*). See the footnote on pages 19-20 for more details.

Ajāmila Ajāmila is the name of a person whose story is told in the *Bhāgavata Purāṇa* (6.1-2). He is the prime example of someone who was saved by using a semblance of the holy name. On his death bed he called for his beloved son whose name was Nārāyaṇa, one of the many names of Viṣṇu. Though he was calling his son and not Lord Nārāyaṇa, he was, as the story goes, freed from the cycle of birth and death and after a short delay was welcomed into Viṣṇu's heaven called Vaikuṇṭha (see below).

bhakti *Bhakti* is the main term in Indic religion for the cultivation of love for the supreme being. *Bhakti* comes from the Sanskrit root $\sqrt{bhaj}$ which means "to partake in," "to divide or share with," "to resort to," "to honor or worship." While *bhakti* can be felt for and practiced with respect to one's parents, other elders, and teachers, it has come to refer primarily to the cultivation and eventual experience of powerful feelings of love for a given deity. In the case of *bhakti* directed to Kṛṣṇa, it is connected with the development of a particular kind of intimate relationship with Kṛṣṇa and with all the complex feelings that go with that relationship.[13] A multivalent term, it is applied to the set of practices that are undertaken as part of the cultivation, to the end result, also called *preman* or love, and in the form of *bhakti-rasa*, to the tasting or enjoyment of that love. Thus, the path of *bhakti* usually begins as a set of practices like hearing the sacred texts and singing or chanting the names of Kṛṣṇa, say, undertaken out of a desire to gain intimacy with him and his dear companions; it then passes through the appearance

[13]There are five recognized relationships according to Rūpa Gosvāmin: peaceful appreciation (*śānta*), servitude (*dāsya*), friendship (*sakhya*), parental affection (*vātsalya*), and erotic attraction (*madhura*, lit. sweet). The degree of intimacy increases with each successive form.

of genuine feeling for or attraction (called *rati*) to the deity in the heart of the practitioner, and culminates in the experience of sacred rapture (*bhakti-rasa* or *preman*), the point at which the love that previously appeared in the heart rises into full consciousness and becomes tasted by the one who possesses it. All of these stages (practice, appearance, and tasting) are referred to as *bhakti* and one who has it in any of its forms is called a *bhakta*.

dharma *Dharma* is one of the most difficult concepts in the Indic tradition to understand and translate. This is partially because it means different things in different contexts and partially because over the centuries it has taken on meanings that it did not originally have. Its most common use these days as the Indian equivalent of "religion" is actually a quite recent and somewhat misleading usage. Another of its modern senses is found in the use of the word *dharma* to mean someone's or something's essential or innate trait or characteristic or nature. This latter turns out to be a blending of a couple of *dharma's* other meanings.

In its earliest usage it meant "that which holds things up or apart." It comes from the Sanskrit root $\sqrt{dhṛ}$, "to hold, bear, carry, maintain." It thus referred to the codes of laws and practices that organized the nascent Hindu society into different social orders or castes and later, after they developed, into the four stages of life. *Dharma* is what held the castes and stages apart, made them distinct, and kept them from getting mixed or blended. Thus, destruction of *dharma* is said to culminate in "mixing" (*saṅkāra*) in the *Bhagavad-gītā*. Since human society in ancient India was never seen as anything but a central part of the functioning of the whole cosmos, observing *dharma* at the same time supported and upheld the whole cosmos. Conversely, failure to observe *dharma* led to a weakening of the cosmos and ushered in or hurried along its destruction.

What one's appropriate *dharma* is is not always easy to tell, especially in times of upheaval and change. India's classic religious text, the *Bhagavad-gītā*, is precisely about this problem and there are many who understand the whole *Mahābhārata*, the Great Epic of India, of which the *Gītā* is but a tiny part, to be about this problem of knowing and observing one's proper *dharma*.

Dharma has two other meanings that create confusion by being unwittingly or even wittingly blended or confused with the one just given. *Dharma* in the philosophical literature means a trait or characteristic of a person or thing. In this sense it is that which is "upheld" by the substratum or substance in which it resides. This when combined with the former meaning of individualized code of conduct creates the idea that *dharma* means one's true or essential trait or nature, that which distinguishes one from all others.

The other meaning is also one that is found in the philosophical texts. There, *dharma* and its opposite, *adharma*, are the results of the pious and impious activities that make up one's "unseen" destiny called the *adṛṣṭa*. Those are the forms through which one's past actions are connected with their appropriate results in the future. They are, according to the school of Nyāya, qualities of the self (*ātman*). Other philosophical schools see them as embodied in the subtle impressions or residual inclinations (*vāsanā*), left in one's deep psyche by past experiences. One carries those experiential residues with one through life in a subtle or psychic body regarded as the vehicle in which the self is carried to its next birth. They thus are one's *karma*.

In this text, *dharma* is most often used in the sense of the religious practice suitable to the current age, the Age of Kali (see below). Thus, in addition to all the other *dharmas*, each age has its own special *dharma* in the sense of a set of religious observances specially effective in that age. The *dharma* of this age is, of course, *saṅkīrtana* of the holy names of Kṛṣṇa, at least according to the Vaiṣṇava texts.

In the context of Caitanya Vaiṣṇava theology, *dharma* means *bhakti* according to Śrī Jīva. As Manindra Nath Babu desmonstrates in his discussion of the eight offense (Chapter 9) Śrī Jīva on the basis of various statements of the *Bhāgavata Purāṇa* habitually takes *dharma* to be synonymous with *bhakti*.

Gaura(hari) "Golden Hari," Hari or Viṣṇu with a golden complexion. This is one of the many names of Śrī Caitanya. Sometimes he is called Gaura, "Golden," Gaurāṅga, "Golden-limbed," and Gauracandra, "Golden Moon."

Goloka/Gokula World of Cows/Herd of Cows. This is Kṛṣṇa's paradise world located far beyond the limits of the material realm. There he lives with his loving companions as an eternal cowherd boy. The Caitanya tradition believes this cowherd form to be Kṛṣṇa's highest form and cowherding his eternal activity. The pastoral planet on which this takes place for all eternity is called Goloka. The basis for these ideas is probably the *Brahma-saṃhitā*, the fifth chapter of which Śrī Caitanya found and copied during his tour of South India. The second verse of that text reads:

> Like a lotus with a thousand petals
> is the great abode called Gokula.
> Its pericarp is his residence
> produced by a portion of his Ananta.[14]

Gokula is practically synonymous with Goloka. There might be a slight distinction made in some texts, but in the *Brahma-saṃhitā* the two seem to be the same. Later, in verses 46 and 52, Goloka is used instead of Gokula. Gokula means a herd of cows or a village of cowherds with a herd of cows.

Govinda A name of Kṛṣṇa: "Possessor of cows." *Go* can have a number of meanings. Cow is the most common meaning and is in fact etymologically related to the word *go*, but it has also been used for the senses and the rays of the sun. The *vind* part of the name is said to come from the root $\sqrt{vid}$, "to find, acquire, procure, possess." Interestingly, the name Govinda might have been brought back into Sanskrit from Prakrit where is was a corrupted form of Gopendra, King of the Cowherds.

Hari A name of Viṣṇu or Kṛṣṇa. The name probably comes from the root $\sqrt{hṛ}$, "to take, bear, carry in or on, carry off or away, steal." Thus, it is often thought to mean the one who carries away one's sins or who steals one's heart. It also means the color yellow or green and might be a reference to the color of the complexion of Viṣṇu or Kṛṣṇa. See the entry for Kṛṣṇa for more details. The root *hṛ* also means "to master, overpower, subdue, conquer, win, win over" and thus the qualities of victory and mastery are applied to Hari.

---

[14]Brahma-saṃhitā, 5.2:

सहस्रपत्रं कमलं गोकुलाख्यं महत्पदम् ।
तत्कर्णिकारं तद्धाम तदनन्तांशसम्भवम् ॥

Ananta is, according to Śrī Jīva, Baladeva, Kṛṣṇa's brother, who on the higher plane is the first expansion of Kṛṣṇa, often depicted as a huge snake with endless heads called Ananta or Śeṣa, and who acts as the facilitating force, manifesting and arranging Kṛṣṇa's eternal abode for Kṛṣṇa's sport. The portion out of which this abode is produced is light, says Jīva.

It might be from this set of meanings that *hari* also came to mean "lion," thus also suggesting that Viṣṇu/Kṛṣṇa occupies the same place among gods and men as lions do in the animal world. A last set of meanings center around ideas like "to enrapture, charm, and fascinate." These powers of fascination too are attributed to the great god Viṣṇu/Kṛṣṇa.

japa Muttering, whispering, repeating. *Japa* is from the root $\sqrt{jap}$ which means "to utter in a low voice." It is one of the ways in which the holy name and the usual way in which other mantras are recited. It is said to be of three types: silent or mental (*mānasika*), whispered (*upāṃśu*), and vocal (*vācika*. In actuality, however, only the second one is really *japa*. The first falls under the scope of "remembering" (*smaraṇa*) and the third is part of *kīrtana*. See Sanātana Gosvāmin's commentary on the *Hari-bhakti-vilāsa* (Play of Devotion to Hari) (11.472).

Kali-yuga This is the last of the four ages that make up a complete cycle in the Hindu conception of time. It lasts 432,000 years according to later Hindu calculations (originally it was only 1200 years) of which approximately 5,000 years have already passed. The complete cycle begins with the Kṛta-yuga or "Age of Fours." It is also called the Satya-yuga, the Age of Truth or "the Golden Age" and represents a time when the world is new and fresh. Peace, prosperity, and religious practice are found in full measure. Life is long and people are good. The Kṛta-yuga lasts four times as long as the Kali-yuga. The next age after Kṛta is the Tretā-yuga, the "Age of Triads." It is three times as long as the Kali-yuga and contains three-fourths of the goodness and truth of the Kṛta-yuga. Then comes the Dvāpara-yuga, the Age of Deuces. It has half of the goodness and truth of the Kṛta-yuga and is twice as long as the Kali-yuga. The Kali-yuga is the last and the worst of the four ages. When it is over the world will be partially destroyed and remade and the cycle will start over again at the top. All together these ages last ten units of time, a unit being equal to the duration of the Kali-yuga. Thus, the whole cycle is 4,320,000 years long. The names of the ages come from the Indian game of dice, the best throw being *kṛta* (four dots), the next best *tretā* (three dots), then *dvāpara* (two dots), and last *kali* (one dot, the losing die). Kali is not to be confused with Kālī, the dark, ferocious goddess of death and protection popular in Bengal, the anger-manifestation of the goddess Durgā.

kīrtana "Mentioning, repeating, saying, telling, praising." It comes from the root $\sqrt{k\bar{\imath}rt}$, "to mention, make mention of, tell, name, call, recite, repeat, relate, declare, communicate, commemorate, celebrate, praise, glorify," and is related to the word *kīrti*, which means "fame." Thus, it means to make famous or spread the fame of someone. Mentioning, repeating, saying, telling, etc. are all ways of doing this. In the context of Vaiṣṇava practice it means to mention, repeat, say, tell of, praise Kṛṣṇa's names, qualities, forms, and activities. As *saṅkīrtana*, or "complete telling," it means to sing of those things to musical accompaniment and according to the Gosvāmins, in groups. Śrī Jīva says that among all the forms of *kīrtana*, loud *kīrtana* of Kṛṣṇa's names is the best.[15] About *saṅkīrtana* he says: "*kīrtana* performed by many people gathered together is called *saṅkīrtana*. And because it leads to a special, astonishing delight it is better than the former (ie. *kīrtana*)."[16] The musical connection is made by Sanātana Gosvāmin when he says that *saṅkīrtana* means the complete or sweet sounding, loud singing of the names of the enjoyer of the Rāsa dance (Kṛṣṇa) with melody and rhythm and so forth.[17] Thus, for the purposes of this text *kīrtana* is the loud repeating or telling of Kṛṣṇa's names, qualities, forms, and activities and *saṅkīrtana* is the loud and musical repeating or telling of Kṛṣṇa's names, qualities, forms, and activities as part of a group.

Kṛṣṇa Kṛṣṇa is the primary name of the god worshipped in the Caitanya tradition. The word *kṛṣṇa* is quite ancient. It is found many times in the oldest of the Vedas, the Rig Veda (15th-10th cents. BCE), but it rarely occurs there as a name. There it means "black, dark, dark-blue" and is often found in opposition to *śukla* and *śveta* which mean "white." It may come from the root $\sqrt{kṛṣ}$ which means "to draw, draw to one's self, drag, pull, drag away, tear; to lead or conduct; to draw into one's power, become master of, overpower." Thus, Kṛṣṇa is often invested with a power of attraction. Kṛṣṇa draws the hearts and minds of all beings away from all else and brings them to himself. The word *kṛṣṇa* may be from another

[15] Bs, para 265: नामसङ्कीर्तनञ्चेदमुच्चैरेव प्रशस्तम्

[16] Bs, 269: अत्र च बहुभिर्मिलित्वा कीर्तनं सङ्कीर्तनमित्युच्यते। तत्तु चमत्कारविशेषपोषात्पूर्वतोऽप्यधिकमिति ज्ञेयम्।

[17] Comm. on Bb, 2.1.21: संकीर्तयन्तीति। तस्य श्रीरासरसिकस्य नाम ये सम्यक् सुस्वरं गाथाबन्धादिनोच्चैर्गायन्तीत्यर्थः।

root, however, the root $\sqrt{kṛś}$ which means "to become lean or thin, emaciated; to cause the moon to wane." This would fit better with the word's meaning as "dark" and its common usage in referring to the dark half of the lunar month (*kṛṣṇa-pakṣa*) when the moon wanes.

Śrī Jīva in his commentary on the *Brahma-saṃhitā* discusses the meaning of the name "kṛṣṇa" after demonstrating on the basis of the construction of certain passages of the *Bhāgavata Purāṇa* that it is the predominant or primary name of the supreme being. Predominance means that all other names are included in it and that it refers to the primary and highest agent of all divine actions and expansions. He cites a verse of unknown original that gives a meaning of the name as follows:

> 'Kṛṣ' is a word that means 'being' (*bhū*) and 'ṇa' means delight (*nirvṛti*). The oneness of those two is the supreme brahman conveyed by the word kṛṣṇa.[18]

Jīva then quotes another, verse from the *Gautamīya Tantra* that has almost the same meaning:

> The word 'kṛṣ' means existence (*sattā*) and 'ṇa' has the nature of joy (*ānanda*). Therefore, happy is the self that consists of being and joy.[19]

After dwelling on some hermeneutic issues, Jīva provides the following explanatory summary:

> The verse from the Gautamīya should be explained in this way. In the first half [of the verse] Kṛṣṇa is [defined as] joy that possesses the power of attracting all. In the second half [it is said that] since he is the joy that attracts all therefore the self [the supreme self, *paramātman*] and the living being find happiness in him. The reason for

[18] Jīva's comm. on Bra. saṃ., 5.1:

कृषिर्भूवाचकः शब्दो णश्च निर्वृतिवाचकः।
तयोरैक्यं परं ब्रह्म कृष्ण इत्यभिधीयते॥

[19] ibid.:

कृषशब्दस्य सत्तार्थो णश्चानन्दस्वरूपकः।
सुखरूपो भवेदात्मा भावानन्दमयस्ततः॥

> that is that the self [both the supreme self and the living being self] consists of the joy of *bhāva* [being, feeling] which is divine love (*preman*). Therefore, the word kṛṣṇa refers to the greatest joy of all that attracts all by its beauty and qualities. And that word applies by convention only to the son of Devakī [Devakīnandana]. His ability to give joy to all is seen in the *Vāsudeva Upaniṣad*: "the son of Devakī gives pleasure to all."[20]

Thus, according to this argument, the fundemental nature pointed to by the name Kṛṣṇa is pleasure or joy that attracts all.

Madanagopāla "Cowherd Cupid." This is another name of Kṛṣṇa. As a cowherd boy (*gopāla*) he is as beautiful and attractive as the god of love (*madana*). *Madana* means "passion" or "the god of love" (aka *Kāmadeva*, Lord of Desire). It is from the root $\sqrt{mad}$ which means "to gladden, exhilarate, intoxicate, animate, inspire." Often times Kṛṣṇa's beauty is said to be greater than millions of gods of love.

Madanagopāla or Madanamohana (Enchanter of the God of Love) is also the name of Sanātana Gosvāmin's image. According to tradition Madanagopāla was given to Sanātana by the wife of Dāmodara Caube, whose house he used to visit when begging for food in Mathurā. Sanātana it is said immediately fell in love with the image. The image is supposed to be one of eight images of Kṛṣṇa that were commissioned and installed around Vraja by Kṛṣṇa's grandson Vajranābha.

Mādhava Another name of Kṛṣṇa. It means "descendant of Madhu" who was an ancestor of the Yādavas, Kṛṣṇa's clan. The city of Mathurā, the ancestral home of the Yādavas, is also called Madhupurī either in honor of that ancestor or because it was founded by him. Thus it can be used of any member of the clan. It is usually used only for Kṛṣṇa, however. It has other resonances that make it specially suited for Kṛṣṇa. Madhu also means "honey," and thus Mādhava means "honeyed" or sweet. Madhu also is the first month of the year in the Hindu calendar (March-April) and thus it

---

[20]ibid.: गौतमीयपद्यञ्चैवं व्याख्येयम्। पूर्वार्द्धे सर्वाकर्षणशक्तिविशिष्ट आनन्दः कृष्ण इत्यर्थः। उत्तरार्द्धे यस्मादेवं सर्वाकर्षकसुखरूपोऽसौ तस्मादात्मा जीवश्च तत्र सुखरूपो भवेत्। तत्र हेतुः। भावः प्रेमा तन्मयानन्दत्वादिति। तदेवं रूपगुणाभ्यां परमबृहत्तमः सर्वाकर्षक आनन्दः कृष्णशब्दवाच्य इति ज्ञेयम्। स च शब्दं श्रीदेवकीनन्द एव रूढः। अस्यैव सर्वानन्दकत्वं वासुदेवोपनिषदि दृष्टम्। देवकीनन्दनो निखिलमानन्दयेदिति।

comes to mean Spring. Mādhava then means related to Spring or vernal. According to one cycle of stories about Kṛṣṇa, the one upon which the lyrical poem, the *Gīta-govinda* of Jayadeva, was based, Kṛṣṇa meets with Rādhā for amorous delights in the Spring and this might also be implied in the name Mādhava. In the mythology, Viṣṇu is also said to have killed a demon named Madhu, but to name someone after a demon he killed seems unlikely. Other of Kṛṣṇa's names like Madhudviṣa (Enemy of Madhu) suggest that meaning.

mañjarī *Mañjarī* means "cluster of blossoms, flower, bud" and is the word applied to what is envisioned in the Caitanya tradition as the eternal female identity of those followers who seek to become the servants of Rādhā and assist her in her amorous love affair with Kṛṣṇa. A *mañjarī* is a young cowherd girl (12-13 years old) who is both a friend and a servant of Rādhā and who prizes Rādhā even over Kṛṣṇa. It is not known who first used the term in this special sense, but it may have been Rūpa Gosvāmin. There is a description of such a female cowherd identity in the *Padma Purāṇa*,[21] but it is not known how early or authentic that passage is. The *mañjarī* identity was later picked up and used extensively by Raghunātha Das Gosvāmin, Kavikarṇapūra, Gopālaguru Gosvāmin, and Kṛṣṇadāsa Kavirāja.

One might view the *mañjarī* metaphorically as a "bud" or "sprout" on the vine of Rādhā. A verse from the great poem of Kṛṣṇadāsa Kavirāja, the *Govinda-līlāmṛta* (Ambrosia of the Sports of Govinda), suggests that there is such a symbiotic relationship between Rādhā and her friends. Kṛṣṇa embraces Rādhā and shivers and goosebumps appear on the bodies of her friends.[22] As both a friend and a servant the *mañjarī* enjoys a certain degree of intimacy with Rādhā that the others who are just friends of Rādhā, called *sakhīs*, don't. The *mañjarī* is also typically younger than Rādhā and the other sakhīs (who are eternally 14-15 years) and thus is able to play a subservient role to them.

The kind of love that a *mañjarī* feels for Rādhā and Kṛṣṇa is defined by Rūpa as *tadbhāvollāsa-rati*, a love that rejoices in their (Rādhā and Kṛṣṇa's) feelings and pleasures. Rūpa defines it in his *Bhakti-*

[21] *Padma Purāṇa*, 5 (Pātāla-khaṇḍa), Chapter 83.
[22] Kṛṣṇadāsa Kavirāja, Gla, 10.12-3.

rasāmṛta-sindh (Ocean of the Ambrosia of the Rasa of Bhakti).[23] See also *preman*.

māyā Kṛṣṇa's creative power. With it he is said to create the material and the non-material worlds. It thus has two varieties. With the external power (*bahiraṅga-śakti*) he creates the material worlds and with the internal power (*antaraṅga-śakti*) he creates the non-material or spiritual worlds. The first is called *māyā* and the second is called *yoga-māyā*. The first is also called ignorance (*avidyā*) and has the effect of covering or hiding Kṛṣṇa from the view of the living beings and the second, called knowledge (*vidyā*), has the effect of revealing or illuminating Kṛṣṇa before them. Coming probably from the root $\sqrt{m\bar{a}}$ which means "to measure," *māyā* produces a measured or delimited reality in which things are defined by clear limits. The immeasurable is measured or delimited by *māyā*, creating the illusion of separateness.

Mukunda Another name of Kṛṣṇa said to mean "Giver of Liberation." This rests on the assumption that *mukum* means liberation (*mukti*). *Da* "to give" in combination with *mukum* thus comes to mean the "giver of liberation." It is doubtful, however, that *mukum* means liberation. Though this is the way the Vaiṣṇava tradition understands the name's meaning, the actual source of the name and its meaning remain unknown. In a clever bending of the infinitely pliable Sanskrit language another meaning is derived for the word in the Caitanya tradition. *Mu* is said to mean the joy of liberation. *Ku* is said to mean "despised, reviled" from the word *kutsita* Thus, *mukum* means that which makes the joy of liberation despised or reviled. This is done by the joy of divine love (*premānanda*). He who gives the joy of divine love which makes the joy of liberation despised is thus Mukunda. In the Caitanya tradition the joy of *bhakti* or *preman* is considered far greater than the joy of liberation.[24]

Nṛsiṃha The "man-lion" descent (*avatāra*) of Kṛṣṇa. Nṛsiṃha appeared out of a pillar to kill the demon Hiraṇyakaśipu who had gained through severe austerities the boons that he would not be killed either in the day or the night, not by man or animal, and not by any weapon. This descent is described in the Seventh Canto of

[23]Rūpa, Brs., 2.5.128.

[24]Based on the commentaries *Bṛhad* and *Saṃkṣepa-vaiṣṇavatoṣanī* on *Bhāg*. 10.10.18.

the *Bhāgavata Purāṇa*, Chapters One through Ten. Nṛsiṃha is regarded as the form of Kṛṣṇa specifically charged with protecting the *bhakta*, devotee of Kṛṣṇa. He was the object of worship of the great child *bhakta* Prahlāda, the son of Hiraṇyakaśipu. See below for more on Prahlāda.

Parīkṣit Mahārāja The grandson of Arjuna, son of Abhimanyu, and the sole survivor of that generation after the surprise night attack on the sleeping grandchildren of the Pāṇḍavas by Aśvatthāman, the son of Droṇa.[25] Parīkṣit survived because he was still in his mother's womb. Even then Aśvatthāman tried to kill him by releasing a Brahman-weapon (*brahmāstra*) on him. It entered into his mother's womb and was about to burn him up when Kṛṣṇa protected him and saved his life. This story of Parīkṣit's salvation is found in the First Canto of the *Bhāgavata Purāṇa*, beginning with Chapter Seven.

King Parīkṣit is the chief hearer of the *Bhāgavata Purāṇa* as it was recited by Śukadeva, the son of Vyāsa. Parīkṣit towards the end of his life had been cursed by an angry *brāhmaṇa* boy to die in seven days by the bite of a snake and he elected to spend that time fasting and listening to Śuka's recitation of the *Bhāgavata*. His name according to some means "he who looks all about" or "the examiner." Alternatively and more probably, it means "he who dwells or rules all around."

Prahlāda The son of the demon Hiraṇyakaśipu who was a devoted follower of Kṛṣṇa. He refused to give up his worship of Kṛṣṇa even when threatened and attacked by his father. Eventually, Nṛsiṃha protected Prahlāda through all of his father's attempts to kill him and then appeared and killed his father. Prahlāda is high in the hierarchy of those who are recipients of the grace of Kṛṣṇa, according to Sanātana Gosvāmin.

preman Sacred or divine love, *preman* or *prīti*, is considered in the Caitanya tradition to be the fifth and highest goal of human life, beyond even liberation from rebirth (the fourth).[26] *Preman* is defined

[25]This episode forms the tenth and shortest book of the *Mahābhārata* called the *Sauptika-parvan* (The Book of the Sleepers or The Book of the Night Attack).

[26]Hindu tradition recognizes four goals of human life (*puruṣārtha*): wealth, pleasure, piety, and liberation. Caitanya Vaiṣṇavism has added to those four a fifth, divine or sacred love.

by Rūpa Gosvāmin in this way: Attraction (ie. delighting in Kṛṣṇa, *kṛṣṇa-rati*), when it becomes condensed or intensified such that it completely melts the heart of its possessor and creates in that person a strong sense of possessiveness towards Kṛṣṇa, is called sacred love. It is a selfless love that is concerned more for the welfare and pleasure of the one loved than for the pleasure of the one loving. It, thus, stands in opposition to lust or selfish love (*kāma*) which seeks self-gratification.

Rādhā Kṛṣṇa's divine lover, she is the highest example of sacred love (*preman*). She among all the cowherd women pleases Kṛṣṇa the most and though not wishing it, she derives the greatest pleasure from loving him. Theologically she is Kṛṣṇa's pleasure power (*hlādinī-śakti*) in person. By connecting with her as her friends and servants (i.e. as *mañjarīs*, see above), others also become capable of pleasing Kṛṣṇa and through her of deriving pleasure from loving Kṛṣṇa. Though not mentioned explicitly in the 10th Canto of the *Bhāgavata Purāṇa* she is considered to be the one special cowherd woman Kṛṣṇa took with him when he disappeared from the rest of the cowherd women who had come to dance with him in the forest of Vṛndāvana during the episode of the circle dance.

Rādhāramaṇa The "enjoyer of Rādhā," a name of Kṛṣṇa that indicates his special erotic relationship with the cowherd woman Rādhā.

rāgānugā (bhakti) "Passion-pursuing" or "passion-following," specially as an adjective for the kind of *bhakti* taught by Śrī Caitanya according to his followers. *Rāgānugā-bhakti* is a form of *bhakti* cultivation that arises from a different source than the "rule-motivated" *bhakti* or *vaidhī-bhakti*, of older forms of Vaiṣṇavism. Passion-pursuing *bhakti* is motived by a desire to develop the kind of passionate love that Kṛṣṇa's dear servants, friends, parents, and lovers have for Kṛṣṇa. It is impelled by a strong desire to love Kṛṣṇa like they do. For this kind of *bhakti* Kṛṣṇa's dear servants, friends, parents, and lovers become the models. Their actions motivated by their love for Kṛṣṇa become the sources of the practices adopted by the practitioner in the cultivation of their kind of *bhakti*.

Rule-initiated *vaidhi-bhakti*, on the other hand, is performed out of a sense of duty, duty instilled by the accepted scriptures or instilled by family and other social institutions. One worships Kṛṣṇa because one's father or mother or earlier ancestors did or because the scriptures one trusts say one should. It is almost the opposite of passionate *bhakti* in which one worships or undertakes practice because one has a strong desire to do so.

rasa Aesthetic rapture. In this text *rasa* is used as shorthand for *bhakti-rasa*, sacred rapture. *Rasa* was a concept developed in Sanskrit aesthetics to describe the aesthetic experience of the connoiseur in enjoying plays and poetry. Abhinavagupta (10th cent. CE) is probably most responsible for bringing the idea of *rasa* to its highest level of sophistication in his commentaries on the *Dhvanyāloka* and especially on the *rasa-sūtra* of the *Nāṭya-śāstra*. Bhojarāja (11th cent. CE), king of Dhārā, developed the idea of *rasa* independently and in a different way. Each writer has his distinct areas of influence, but Abhinavagupta's understanding of *rasa* came to be regarded as the mainstream tradition. Rūpa Gosvāmin, following the lead of several predecesors, took the idea of *rasa* and applied it to religious experience, surprisingly relying more on Bhojarāja's understanding than on Abhinavagupta's. The result was his version of the idea of *bhakti-rasa*, sacred rapture, which became dominantly influential in the later Caitanya Vaiṣṇava tradition and in other Vaiṣṇava traditions as well.

One experiences sacred rapture when one's feeling (*bhāva*), that is, delight in Kṛṣṇa (*kṛṣṇa-rati*), is brought to the level of enjoyment or tastiness by means of the excitants (*vibhāvas*), consequents (*anubhāvas*), and transient emotions (*vyabhicāribhāvas*). The feeling of delight in Kṛṣṇa is, according to the Caitanya tradition, outside the natural (*alaukika*), and it appears in the mind of a practitioner at some point in his or her development in *bhakti* and becomes part of his mind. Then when the practitioner encounters the excitants, consequents, and transients in literature, drama, or song, that delight is transformed into joy. Since *preman* is an intensified or condensed form of delight in Kṛṣṇa, the threshold for the transition of delight into joy becomes dramatically lowered. Then the mere sight of a peacock feather or a bluish rain cloud can send a person with *preman* into sacred rapture.

saṅkīrtana See *kīrtana*.

smaraṇa Remembering or recollecting. This refers to a Caitanya Vaiṣṇava practice that is more of a form of meditation or visualization than it is a "remembering." Its practitioners have never experienced what they are "remembering." So for them it is not remembering at all. What they are really doing is focused thinking about Kṛṣṇa and what he and his various companions are doing at any particular moment of the day. Thus, remembering is based on the idea that Kṛṣṇa is engaged in an eternal sport which is taking place daily in Kṛṣṇa's paradise, Goloka. The day is divided into eight periods and Kṛṣṇa's activities in each of those periods is "remembered" in the corresponding period of the practitioner's day. Thus, when Kṛṣṇa is in the bower with Rādhā at the end of the night and must be awakened and returned to his home before his mother discovers he is missing, the practitioner "remembers" or visualizes it, placing himself in the action in a mentally conceived or imagined body (usually but not always that of a *mañjarī*) given to him by his guru. A number of poetic works have been composed by followers of Caitanya to help the practitioner in this process of creative remembering. The longest and most detailed is the *Govinda-līlāmṛta* (Ambrosia of the Sports of Govinda) by Kṛṣṇadāsa Kavirāja.

śravaṇa Hearing or listening. Hearing is the first stage in the practice of *bhakti*. It means hearing from the guru, the scriptures, and other Vaiṣṇava about Kṛṣṇa, his names, his qualities, his forms, and his sports. Hearing if done well, it is said, will destroy the impurities or diseases of the heart and mind and clear the way for the descent of *bhakti* into them.

Sūta Gosāi (Goswami) This is the outer reciter of the *Bhāgavata Purāṇa*. He was present when the text was recited for Parīkṣit by Śuka, the inner reciter, in the presense of the author Vyāsa himself. Later, he recites the text for Śaunaka and the other sages in the forest of Naimiṣaraṇya. Sūta's recitation is the outer textual frame that surrounds the inner textual frame that consists of the recitation of Śuka.

turīya The "fourth." In this text it means the highest position in any hierarchy. Originally it was used in the Upaniṣads to indicate the "fourth" state of consciousness, the state of the pure self, beyond the states of waking, dream, and deep sleep. Later it came to mean the highest thing in any hierarchy involving four items.

vaidhī (bhakti) See *rāgānugā* above.

Vaikuṇṭha Kṛṣṇa's lower heaven. Vaikuṇṭha is the place where Kṛṣṇa's majestic aspect is manifested. Complementing his majesty is his sweetness (*mādhurya*) or intimate aspect which is manifest in his higher heaven called Goloka (see above). In Vaikuṇṭha Kṛṣṇa reigns as Viṣṇu with four arms and all the majesty and opulence of a super-cosmic king. Those who worship Kṛṣṇa by means of rule-motivated *bhakti* (*vaidhi-bhakti*) are said to go to Vaikuṇṭha after gaining success. Those who worship by passion-motivated *bhakti* (*rāgānuga-bhakti*) instead go to Goloka.

Vrajendranandana The son of the king of Vraja, another name of Kṛṣṇa. The king of Vraja, the pasture lands, is Nanda the cowherd and Yaśodā is his wife. Kṛṣṇa is referred to as Nanda's son, though according to the story of his birth, Kṛṣṇa was actually born as the son of Vasudeva because of which he was known as Vāsudeva. To protect him from the evil king Kaṃsa, Vasudeva carried him on the night of his birth to the village of Nanda and swapped him for Nanda's new-born girl. Along these same lines, Kṛṣṇa is also often called Nandanandana and Yaśodānandana

Authors Cited

Īśvara Purī (15th-16th centuries) He was a disciple of Mādhavendra Purī and the *mantra* guru of Śrī Caitanya. Śrī Caitanya met him in Gayā when Caitanya was there to offer post-mortem rites for his father. Śrī Caitanya underwent a powerful conversion experience at Gayā and Īśvara Purī guided him into the world of Vaiṣṇavism. He is said to have written a book called the *Kṛṣṇa-līlāmṛta* (Ambrosia of the Sports of Kṛṣṇa) which is now lost but for a few stray verses.

Jīva Gosvāmin (1508-?) Śrī Jīva is the nephew of Sanātana and Rūpa Gosvāmin. Under their guidance and tutelage he wrote some of the most important works on Caitanya Vaiṣṇava theology, called the *Ṣaṭ-sandarbha,* the Six Treatises. After the passing of his uncles he became the leader of the Caitanya Vaṣṇṇava community in Vṛndāvana.

Kavi Karṇapūra (1524?-?) Karṇapūra was the son of Śivānanda Sena, one of the close married followers of Śrī Caitanya. His other name was Paramānanda Sena. He wrote a number of important works in the realms of both literature and literary criticism. He is most famous for his works on the life of Śrī Caitanya, a poem written when he was still quite young (16 years) called the *Caitanya-caritāmṛta Mahākāvya* (Ambrosia of the Life of Caitanya) and a play written much later and called the *Caitanya-candrodaya Nāṭaka* (Rise of the Moon of Caitanya) (1573 CE).

Kṛṣṇadāsa Kavirāja (1518-1612) He was a member of the second generation of Caitanya Vaiṣṇavas in Vṛndāvana who were trained and groomed by the six primary Gosvāmins and their associates. Kṛṣṇadāsa Kavirāja never met Śrī Caitanya himself, nor probably Śrī

Nityānanda either. The latter, however, Kṛṣṇadāsa Kavirāja says appeared to him in a dream and ordered him to go to Vṛndāvana to assist the Gosvāmins there. It is said that in recognition of his extraordinary accomplishment in writing the longest poem on Kṛṣṇa's sports ever written, the *Govinda-līlāmṛta* (Ambrosia of the Sports of Kṛṣṇa), Śrī Jīva gave him the title Kavirāja (King of Poets). His other masterpiece was the biography of Śrī Caitanya called the *Caitanya-caritāmṛta* (Ambrosia of the Life of Caitanya). This Bengali biography built on the materials of the previous biographies and, incorporating in addition eye-witness accounts of and insights into Śrī Caitanya's last days in Purī and the essential thoughts and insights of the Gosvāmins of Vṛndāvana, became the main vehicle for the dissemination of the Caitanya movement in Bengal.

Narottama Dāsa Ṭhākura (16th century) Another member of the younger generation of Caitanya Vaiṣṇavas in Vṛndāvana who wrote numerous songs and works in Bengali that have been a central force in the spreading of the Caitanya tradition in Bengal. His *Prema-bhakti-candrikā* (Moonlight on the Bhakti of Love) and *Prārthanā* (Prayers) have remained enormously popular and are part of the daily reading, singing, and study of countless Caitanya Vaiṣṇavas even today. Narottama Dāsa Ṭhākura along with Śrīnivāsācārya and Śyāmānada Dāsa were sent by Śrī Jīva Gosvāmin with all of the manuscripts of the writings of the Gosvāmins of Vṛndāvana to Bengal so that they could be copied and distributed.

Prabodhānanda Sarasvatī (15th-16th centuries) An immediate follower of Śrī Caitanya, he wrote several works on Caitanya Vaiṣṇavism. He is most famous for his elaborate praise of Śrī Caitanya in his work called the *Caitanya-candrāmṛta* (Ambrosia of the Moon of Caitanya). Some think that he was the Advaitin sannyāsin that Śrī Caitanya is said to have defeated in Vārāṇasī named Prakāśānanda Sarasvatī, and that as a result of his conversion to Caitanya's view he changed his name to Prabodhānanda. It is more likely that he was an uncle of Gopāla Bhaṭṭa Gosvāmin from South India who was converted to Caitanya's views when Caitanya went on pilgrimage there. He was the *śikṣā* or teaching guru of Gopāla Bhaṭṭa.

Raghunātha Dāsa Gosvāmin (16th century) He is counted as one of the six Gosvāmin of Vṛndāvana, the only non-*brāhmaṇa* among them. He wrote several works and stotras that are highly regarded in Caitanya Vaiṣṇavism today. He was with Śrī Caitanya in Purī during much of his final stay there. Śrī Caitanya placed him under the care of his close follower Svarūpa Dāmodara and it was through Raghunātha Dāsa that the Vṛndāvana circle was exposed to Svarūpa Dāmodara's interpretation of the true nature and purpose of Śrī Caitanya's descent. Born the son of a rich man, he rejected his father's wealth and status to live a life of poverty and detachment in order to follow Śrī Caitanya.

Rūpa Gosvāmin (1470-1557 C.E.) He was the younger brother of Sanātana Gosvāmin, uncle of Śrī Jīva Gosvāmin, and the Caitanya tradition's finest poet, dramatist, and literary critic. His works on *bhakti-rasa*, the *Bhakti-rasāmṛta-sindhu* (Ocean of the Ambrosia of Sacred Rapture) and the *Ujjvala-nīlamaṇi* (Blazing Sapphire), are the defining texts on that topic. He laid the groundwork for the practice of *smaraṇa*, remembering (see above), and encouraged the younger generation of Caitanya Vaiṣṇavas in Vṛndāvana to further develop it. With his older brother Sanātana, he was at the center of the circle of Caitanya Vaiṣṇavas in Vṛndāvana.

Sanātana Gosvāmin (1465-1555 C.E.) The "father" of Caitanya Vaiṣṇava theology. Without Sanātana Gosvāmin's contribution Caitanya's movement would have remained mostly sentimental fluff. He gave it direction and substance. His younger brother Rūpa gave it wings and the ability to fly and his nephew Śrī Jīva gave it muscle and insight. They all three kept Caitanya's movement from remaining a mostly regional religious movement and transformed it into a tradition of pan-Indian importance and influence. Sanātana's major work was his *Bṛhad-bhāgavatāmṛta* (Great Ambrosia of Bhaktas of the Lord). His final work, the extensive commentary on the 10th Canto of the *Bhāgavata Purāṇa*, the *Bṛhad-vaiṣṇava-toṣaṇī* (Great Pleaser of Vaiṣṇavas) is also a masterpiece of Vaiṣṇava hermeneutics and theology.

Viśvanātha Cakravartin (1650-? C.E.) He was a great writer and commentator who lived in the second half of the 17th century. He commented upon almost all of the major Caitanya Vaiṣṇava texts and wrote several original works of his own. In this book his commentary on the *Bhāgavata Purāṇa* is cited frequently. His commentaries on Rūpa's *Bhakti-rasāmṛta-sindhu* (Ocean of the Ambrosia of Sacred Rapture) and *Ujjvala-nīlamaṇi* (Blazing Sapphire) are also considered fundamentally important. Sometimes his literary talent which is considerable is compared with that of Rūpa Gosvāmin. Some even go so far as to refer to him as a reincarnation of Rūpa.[27] Viśvanātha Cakravartin is considered an authority on interpreting the intentions of the Gosvāmin.

[27]It is odd that in Caitanya Vaiṣṇavism and indeed in Hinduism in general, no one seems to be allowed to be too good. If someone is recognized as excellent in some way in Caitanya Vaiṣṇṇavism, he is immediately identified with some other earlier good writer or thinker or sage. So the credit goes to that earlier writer or sage, not to the one who actually deserves it. Within Hinduism in general it seems as if Vyāsa has written everything: the *Mahābhārata*, all the Purāṇas, the *Vedānta-sūtras*. This tendency to collapse many persons into one seems like an ancient and deep-rooted one in Hindu culture.

Bibliography of Works Consulted

Bhaktivinoda, Saccidānanda (1963), *Śrī Hari-nāma-cintāmaṇi*, fifth edn, Jagajjāvan Dās Bhaktiśāstrī, Kṛṣṇanagara, Nadīyā.

Das, Raghava Chaitanya (1954), *Divine Name*, first edn, Raghava Chaitanya Das, Bombay.

Gosvāmin, Rūpa (G488 [1974]), *Laghu-bhāgavatāmṛta*, second edn, Caitanya Math.

Gosvāmin, Rūpa (G495 [1981]), *Bhakti-rasāmṛta-sindhu*, third edn, Haribol Kuthīra.

Gosvāmin, Sanātana (G458 [1944]), *Bṛhad-bhāgavatāmṛta*, first edn, Śacīnātharāya, Mayamanasiṃha.

Goswami, Kanupriya (1989), *Śrī Śrī Nāma Cintāmaṇi*, Vol. 3, first edn, Sri Kishor Ray Goswami, Nabadwip.

Goswami, Kanupriya (1992), *Śrī Śrī Nāma Cintāmaṇi*, Vol. 1, fourth edn, Sri Kishor Ray Goswami, Nabadwip.

Goswami, Kanupriya (1993), *Śrī Śrī Nāma Cintāmaṇi*, Vol. 2, second edn, Sri Kishor Ray Goswami, Nabadwip.

Goswami, Kanupriya (1999), *The Dawn of the Age of Love*, second edn, Sri Gaurray Goswami, Calcutta.

Guha, Manindranath ([1969]), *Śrī Mādhava Mādhurya Mañjuṣā*, first edn, Sāvitrī Guha, Vṛndāvana.

Guha, Manindranath ([1971]), *Śrī Gaurakaruṇā-candrikā-kaṇā*, first edn, Sāvitrī Guha, Pānihāṭi, 24 Paragaṇā.

Guha, Manindranath ([1984]*a*), *Śrī Caitanya-śikṣāṣṭaka*, second edn, Sāvitrī Guha, Vṛndāvana.

Guha, Manindranath ([1984]*b*), *Śrīman-nāmāmṛtasindhubindu*, second edn, Sāvitrī Guha, Vṛndāvana.

Kapoor, O.B.L. (1997), *The Companions of Sri Chaitanya Mahaprabhu*, first edn, Srila Badrinarayana Bhagavata Bhushana Prabhu, Radha Kunda, Vrindavana.

Majumdara, Vimanavihari (1959), *Śrīcaitanyacaritera Upādāna*, second edn, Kalikātā Viśvavidyālaya, Kalikātā (West Bengal, India).

Prabodhānanda Sarasvatī (Manindranath Guha, ed. & trans.) (1971), *Śrīśrīcaitanya-candrāmṛtam*, first edn, Sāvitrī Guha, Pānihāṭi, 24 Paragaṇā.

Vidyāvinoda, Sundarananda (1961), *Śrī Nāmācintāmaṇi Kiraṇa Kaṇikā*, first edn, Navīnakṛṣṇa Dāsa, Śrī Dhāma Navadvīpa (West Bengal, India).

Vyāsa (1945), *Śrīmadbhāgavatam*, Vol. 1-3, first edn, Śacīnātharāya-caturdhurīṇa, Mayamanasiṃha (East Bengal, now Bangla Desh).

Notes

Notes

www.ingramcontent.com/pod-product-compliance
Lightning Source LLC
Chambersburg PA
CBHW021828020426
42334CB00014B/534
* 9 7 8 0 9 7 4 7 9 6 8 1 9 *